Memorable Places
Among
The Holy Hills

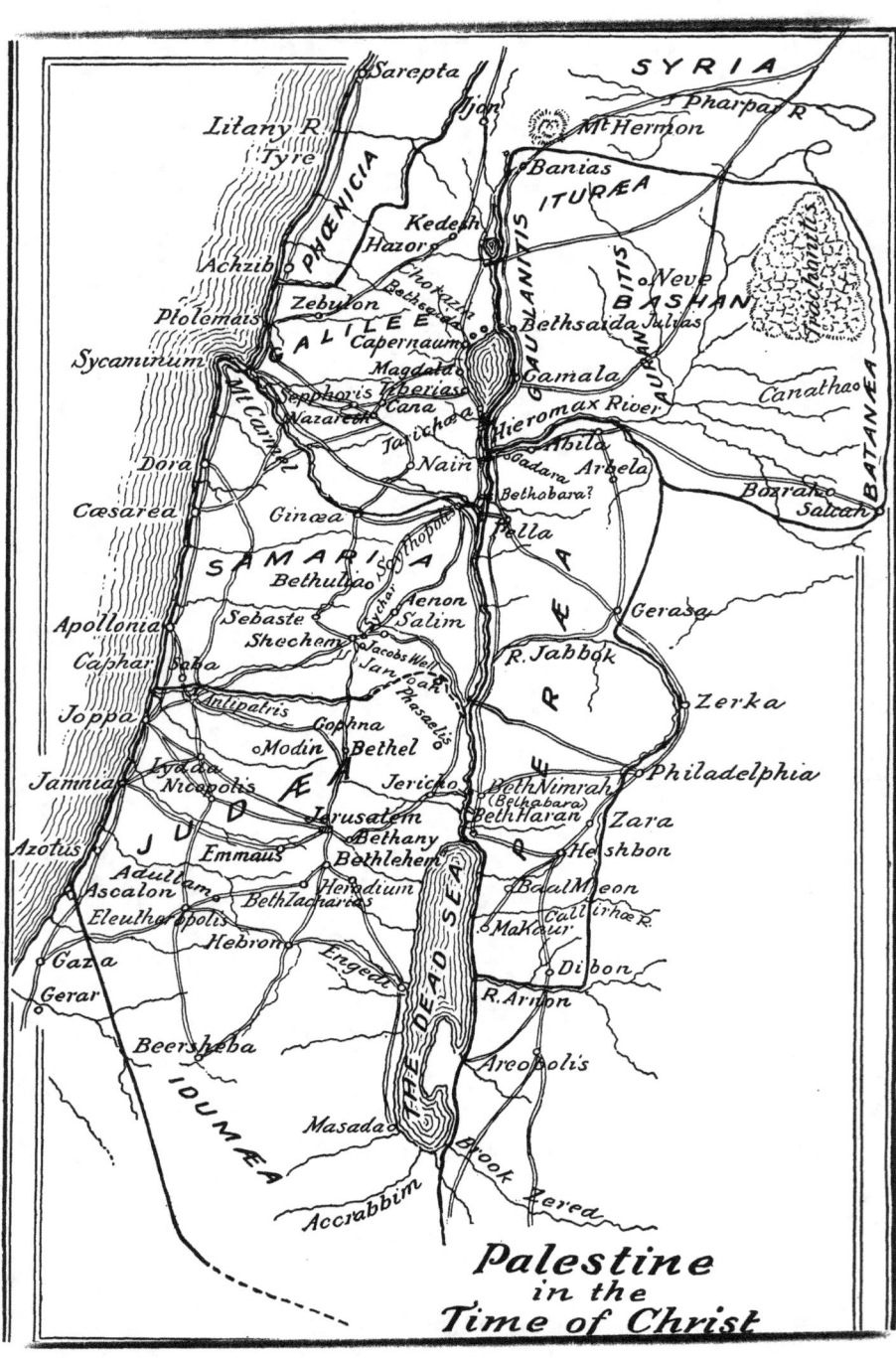

Memorable Places
Among
The Holy Hills

By
ROBERT LAIRD STEWART, D. D.
Professor of Pastoral Theology and Biblical Archæology in the Theological Seminary of Lincoln University, Penna.

WIPF & STOCK · Eugene, Oregon

Wipf and Stock Publishers
199 W 8th Ave, Suite 3
Eugene, OR 97401

Memorable Places Among the Holy Hills
By Stewart, Robert Laird
Softcover ISBN-13: 978-1-5326-1602-0
Hardcover ISBN-13: 978-1-5326-1603-7
eBook ISBN-13: 978-1-7252-3809-1
Publication date 12/9/2016
Previously published by Revell, 1902

TO MY WIFE

Preface

THE places described in this series of sketches are those which come into view most frequently and prominently in connection with the Story of Redemption.

The purpose has been to give in brief space and popular form, the most accurate and interesting information obtainable from the accumulations of the past and the records of recent investigation and discovery: as well as from the impressions gained from personal study and observation.

It is a significant fact that Palestine—the homeland of the Bible—is engaging the attention of the Christian world as never before in its history: and, as a result, there is a growing demand for helpful and easily accessible information concerning it. While many travellers and writers with clear vision and descriptive powers of a high order have passed this way hitherto, there are still new discoveries to be announced, new impressions to be recorded; and the story of its memorable places, interlinked, as they are, with the sweetest story ever heard in earth or heaven, will still be told and retold with growing interest from generation to generation.

The illustrations which cover the whole

ground have been carefully selected as supplementary aids to the descriptions of the text.

Credit for photographic views reproduced by permission and for helpful information and suggestion from various sources, has been given in the body of the work.

        LINCOLN UNIVERSITY, PA.

Sept. 1st, 1902.

Contents

	PAGE
INTRODUCTION. RECENT RESEARCHES IN THE HOLY LAND	9

I
HEBRON,—THE RESTING-PLACE OF THE PATRIARCHS 27

II
BETHLEHEM,—THE BIRTH-PLACE OF JESUS . . 43

III
NAZARETH,—THE HOME OF JESUS . . . 55

IV
THE WILDERNESS OF JUDEA 72

V
SHECHEM AND ITS ENVIRONS 86

VI
THE PLAIN OF GENNESARET 97

VII
THE SEA OF GALILEE 107

Contents

VIII "His Own City"	118
IX Bethsaida of Galilee	128
X The Mountain of the Transfiguration	139
XI The Place of "The Noble Sanctuary"	148
XII The Pool of Siloam	180
XIII The Way to Jericho	193
XIV The Fords of the Jordan	203
XV The Land Beyond Jordan	214
XVI The Strongholds of Machærus and Masada	225

List of Maps and Illustrations

	Facing Page
MAP OF PALESTINE IN THE TIME OF CHRIST	Title
THE NEW ENTRANCE BESIDE THE JAFFA GATE, JERUSALEM	10
HEBRON AND ITS ENVIRONS	28
ABRAHAM'S OAK IN THE VALE OF MAMRE	30
BETHLEHEM OF JUDEA	44
NAZARETH, THE HOME OF JESUS	56
DRY BED OF WATERFALL IN WADY DABR	72
THE GREEK CONVENT OF MAR SABA	76
SHECHEM AND ITS ENVIRONS	86
SEA OF GALILEE	98
SITE OF MAGDALA—THE HOME OF MARY MAGDALENE	104
NORTHERN BASIN OF GENNESARET FROM HIGHLANDS OF GALILEE	108
TIBERIAS BY THE SEA OF GALILEE	114
ROCK CLIFF AND FOUNTAIN (Ain et Tin) AT KHAN MINYEH	126
BETHSAIDA OF GALILEE (Ain Tabighah)	132
SOURCE OF THE JORDAN AT BANIAS	144
THE MOSQUE OF EL AKSA—TEMPLE AREA	148
THE DOME OF THE ROCK AND ITS ASSOCIATED BUILDINGS	152

LIST OF MAPS AND ILLUSTRATIONS
(*Continued*)

South Wall of the Temple Area . . .	164
Sketch Plan of Recent Excavations in and about the Port of Siloam .	180
The Jordan Bridge at Mouth of Wady Shaib (Nimrim Ford)	212
Portion of Wall and Gateway of Northern Edge of Summit of the Hill of Masada .	232

INTRODUCTION

RECENT RESEARCHES IN THE HOLY LAND

PREEMINENT among the lands of Sacred Story is the narrow strip, inland of the Mediterranean Sea, which for long ages has borne the distinctive title of "The Holy Land." It is a rugged and singularly diversified tract, and yet throughout its whole extent it is a *unity* in its physical conformation. It is not a domain of uncertain area, whose metes and bounds were determined in different periods by political changes or revolutions, but by divine allotment it became the peculiar heritage of Israel, and in the title deed of its transfer its limits are carefully defined. On the one hand, its border is the sea; on the other the desert. Northward its boundary is the wide break between the Lebanon and the Nusairiyeh Mountains, designated as the "Entering in of Hamath"; southward it extends to the "River, or Brook, of Egypt," a long, shallow wady or watercourse, which runs in a northwesterly direction, through a portion of the wilderness of Israel's wanderings, and enters the Mediterranean Sea a short distance south of the two pillars erected by Mehemet Ali, to mark the boundary between Asia and Africa. Thus on every side, except the north, it is bordered by a wide expanse of sea or desert. The extent of this Greater Palestine from north to south is 290 miles. Its area is not less than 25,000 square miles. To this land in its entirety belong the glowing descriptions, poetic illusions and hallowed associations which have given to it its world-wide fame and exclusive title. Here as nowhere else the Almighty has manifested His glory and unfolded His purpose of redeeming grace. "Its hills and valleys have been transfigured by meanings and mysteries mightier than physical influences," and over it all there shines a light that fades not, but grows more radiant with the ages. It is the land of the Patriarchs; of the Prophets; of the Sacred Poets; of the Apostles; of the world renowned Kings, David and Solomon; and of a host of saintly men and women whose names are familiar as household words. But more than all it is the land where the Son of God was made flesh and dwelt among men:

> "Here lie those holy fields
> O'er whose acres walked those blessed feet,
> Which 1900 years ago were nailed
> For our advantage to the bitter cross."

A half century ago the principal sources of information concerning the Holy Land were doubtful assumptions based upon medieval traditions, or the scarcely more reliable impressions and generalizations of travellers, who flitted hastily from point to point throughout the East. In many cases the traditional rubbish which had

THE NEW ENTRANCE BESIDE THE JAFFA GATE, JERUSALEM.
To the right is the Tower of Hippicus and the recently erected Fountain. This break in the wall was made for the entrance of Emperor William of Germany.

Introduction

gathered around the sacred sites of Palestine was more perplexing to the real explorer than the heaps of débris from walls and ruined strongholds. Happily for us, this is true no longer. The work of exploration on a strictly scientific basis, commenced by Dr. Edward Robinson—the father of Palestinian geography nearly sixty years ago—has been carried on by a worthy corps of successors, who, amid many discouragements and perils, have given years of patient study and investigation to the identification of places, the retracing of old boundary lines, the translation of ancient names and records, the excavation of long buried cities and the survey of the land as a whole. The most important results have been secured within the last twenty years in connection with the explorations and accurate triangulation surveys undertaken by the Palestine Exploration Fund. During the progress of this work a list of 10,000 names was collected and 172 Biblical sites were discovered. At the present time, 434 out of the 622 Biblical names west of the Jordan have been identified with a reasonable degree of probability. As the outcome of this important work we now have a relief map covering most of the land; and a series of beautifully executed wall maps as accurate as the ordnance map of England. The actual recovery of the old lines of the tribal divisions west of the Jordan, by retracing the natural features of the country, which unquestionably have remained without change; and the identification of long forgotten sites along these lines, by names which, with slight changes, have clung to them since the days of Joshua, may be justly regarded as one of the most noteworthy achievements of the survey party. This recovery is owing mainly to the fact that the original divisions were made to conform, as far as possible, to the natural features of the country. It implies on the part of Joshua's corps of surveyors a clear and accurate knowledge of the details of its physiographic features, as well as a general knowledge of its configuration and adaptations. It also furnishes a strong incidental proof in support of the claim that the record which defines these boundaries with such painstaking fidelity, was written at the time when this allotment—itself a matter of history—was actually made. It seems incredible that it should have been regarded of so much value as to occupy the space of ten chapters in the book of Joshua, if it had been written at any period after the displacement or separation of the tribes. It is evident, also, that the confusion of lines by the events of subsequent history, and the formation of new political divisions, would have made the task of preparing such a record a work of superhuman wisdom, as wonderful in its reach backward as the sweep of the inspired prophet's vision forward into the future.

"These facts," says Colonel Conder, "serve assuredly to prove that the geography of the Book of Joshua is no idle tale, but a real division of a real country, capable of the most minute

Introduction

critical examination by aid of the most scientific modern research."

In the light of all this patient and continuous investigation and discovery, the geography of the Holy Land has become a study of absorbing interest. It has furnished a clue to the explanation of many historical difficulties; filled old words with new meanings; revealed correspondences with the Bible hitherto unseen; corroborated minute circumstances of position, time and distance incidentally given by the sacred writers; and, in a word, has restored the real historic setting of a series of real historic narratives.

Looking at the land as a whole—as it now appears—we find many things in connection with its location, framework and physical features which are absolutely unique; and which we believe can only be explained satisfactorily on the assumption that it was a land marvellously fashioned and adapted to all the conditions of its marvellous history.

1. *Its Position Among the Nations.*—Palestine had the singular distinction of being at the centre of the civilization and influence of the ancient world. Its coast plain has been the great international highway and war-path of the nations for upwards of 5,000 years. Canaan was the "Westland" of the Babylonians and Assyrians, towards which a restless tide of immigration had been flowing long before the days of Abraham. It was the Midland region of the Egyptians, through which their armies and caravan bands of

necessity must pass on the way to the rich plains and valleys of the East. It was the "High Bridge," as Ritter terms it, on which the legions which followed Alexander, or the great generals of Rome, ascended or descended respectively into the basin of the Nile or the Euphrates. It was, in a word, *the meeting-place of three continents and three great civilizations.*

While occupying this important position, the main portion of the country west of the Jordan was an immense rock-buttressed stronghold, whose gateways to the plain on either hand were long defiles, or narrow passes, easily defended against the hosts of an invading army. This was especially true of the rugged section of the central range which lies to the south of the plain of Esdraelon—the scene of most of the great events in the history of Israel. This closely compacted block of mountain territory extends to the vicinity of Beersheba, a distance of ninety miles, and fills up most of the space between the sea and the Jordan. It is almost encircled by a lowland belt, so that it is possible to pass around from the head of the Dead Sea by way of the Jordan Valley, the Esdraelon and coast plains, and the lower levels of the South country to Engedi—a short distance from the starting point—without crossing a mountain ridge or ascending a prominent elevation.

The Land of Israel, as a whole, except the coast plain, was also isolated from the nations around, as already stated, by physical features of unusual character and combination. The sea, the wilderness, the desert, and the towering mountains of Lebanon—each in its place—were barriers against sudden attack or invasion from without.

This double relation of exclusion and ready intercommunication, paradoxical as it may seem, was a necessary feature in the heritage of a people, who were at one period of their history to *dwell apart* from the nations, and at another to carry the message of life and salvation to *all* the nations of the earth. It was fitting, also, that the Book, which contained this message, should be given in a land which touched all lands.

2. *The Exceptional Physical Features of the Land.*—The surface of the country is naturally divided into four longitudinal sections, viz.: The maritime plain, the twin mountain ranges, known as Lebanon and Anti-Lebanon, and the deeply-cleft valley which lies between them. In briefest outline, the prominent physical features are: *Two parallel mountain ranges* and *two corresponding depressions, all running north and south throughout the extent of the land.* Each of these sections contributes an indispensable part to the peculiar formation of the country, giving to it a *universal* character, which no other country possesses, within such limited compass, on the face of the earth. The Lebanon range is corrugated on both sides by deep wadies, and in general may be designated as a back-bone ridge.

South of the head waters of the Jordan it seldom rises to the height of 3,000 feet, but in the north its snow-clad summits at some points are more than 10,000 feet above the sea. The Anti-Lebanon as a whole presents a broader surface on its summit, and culminates in the snow-covered heights of Mount Hermon, 9,383 feet above the sea. The valley, or cleft between these mountain ridges, has been fitly characterized as a phenomenon unique on the earth's surface. Nowhere on its wrinkled face do we find a furrow so deep, or so remarkable for its length, directness and rapid descent. Between the Lebanons it is a deep basin, eighty miles long and four to nine wide, rimmed in by mountain walls 5,000 or 6,000 feet high. In the southern portion the valley sinks from sea level to a depression 1,300 feet below, in a distance of less than 100 miles. If to this we add the lower level of the Dead Sea basin, the depression is 2,600 feet, or nearly one-half of a mile towards the centre of the earth. Putting it in another form, "a man who stands at the margin of the Dead Sea is almost as far below the ocean surface as the miner in the lowest depths of any mine." Says Dr. Smith: "There may be something on the surface of another planet to match the Jordan Valley; there is nothing on this. No other part of our earth, uncovered by water, sinks 300 feet below the level of the ocean."

From the summit of the Mount of Olives to the lowest depths of the Dead Sea basin the depression is 5,200 feet. If a plummet were dropped from a level corresponding with the summit of Olivet to this depth, it would require the paying out of a line nearly a mile long; and yet the distance between these points is less than twenty miles.

These statements can only give a partial view of the most striking physiographic features of the heritage of Israel, viewed as a whole. Within its limits it is scarcely possible to conceive of any variation or peculiarity of land formation that is not represented. Here may be found in close juxtaposition sea and desert; Alpine heights and phenomenal depths; fertile plans and barren wilderness; rolling downs and upland pastures; terraced slopes and deeply scarred lava beds; park-like stretches and bleakest moorlands; valleys of Edenic beauty and dark cañons, suggestive of the shades of death; rivers and lakes; snow-clad heights and depths of tropical heat and luxuriance; ice-bound streams and steaming fountains; shady glens and interminable wadies; open glades and impenetrable jungles of cane and papyrus—in short, every feature of nature's diversified handiwork, which is suggestive of the beautiful, the picturesque or the sublime.

The variations of climate correspond with these variations in physical features. The sea, the desert, and the extraordinary range of levels are the most potent influences in effecting these variations, which range from Alpine cold to torrid heat. From the summit of Lebanon to the low levels of the Jordan Valley all the zones and climes of the earth, with the flora and fauna peculiar to each, are represented. As the Arabs have happily expressed it: "Lebanon bears winter on its head, spring on its shoulders, and autumn in its lap, while summer lies at its feet." In a single day Canon Tristram rode on horseback through four different zones of plant and animal life, passing from the region of Scotch firs on Mount Gilead to the region of the date palms in the plains of the Jordan. From the snow fields of Hermon to the lowest levels of the Jordan Valley is less than 100 miles; and yet in the one perpetual winter abides; in the other there is never a trace of snow or hoarfrost. Between wheat harvest in the Jordan Valley and on the plateau of Jerusalem there is an interval of about four weeks, while the distance between is scarcely more than sixteen miles.

The feat of Beniah, who went down and slew a lion in the midst of a pit in the time of snow, is referred to by Dr. Smith as an illustration of the remarkable variation of climate within distances but a few miles apart. To this he adds the statement: "The beast had strayed up the Judean hills from Jordan and had been caught in a sudden snow-storm. Where else than Palestine could lions and snow thus come together?"

3. *The close correspondence between the Land and the Book, and the manifest correspondence of places with the events described*, have been

Introduction

greatly multiplied, and have grown more wonderful every year as the result of modern investigation. In such works as the "Researches" of Dr. Robinson, or the "Land and the Book," by Dr. Thomson, who spent more than forty years of his life amid the scenes he has so graphically described, there are proofs and illustrations abundant, striking and minute of the connection between the locality avowedly chosen of God, for the unfolding of His purpose of grace, and the Book in which this revelation is made known.

Its rugged framework is the setting of the Bible, and correspondences such as these are found all over the face of the land. It is the mold into which Scripture truth and historic detail have been cast for every nation and for all time, and wherever tested the one answers to the other as the die to its impress. To understand the story of Gettysburg, one must have before him an outline picture of the field on which the battle was fought. Its situation and configuration must be known before the history of the great conflict can be intelligently comprehended. So of every other event. If we have the setting we can understand the story. It takes on definiteness and coloring and lifelikeness as it is connected with the details of its environment. To the ordinary reader of the Bible the mention of a place called Dothan in the story of Joseph's life suggests little or nothing of special interest, but when we come to know it as a mountain-rimmed plain of rare beauty, sought out to-day by the shepherds when other pastures fail; when we find it on the track worn by the merchantmen of the East for something like 5,000 years; when we learn that there are empty cisterns now, near to this great highway, like that one in which Joseph was imprisoned by his brethren; when we find near by a perennial spring, around which Joseph's brethren probably sat as he drew near, and we trace down the wady leading out from this plain the ancient road to Egypt—the name and story are associated with *living realities* of undying interest, and imagination truthfully and vividly reproduces the scene. The narrative of Jesus at the well of Jacob may be told with profit, without reference to the place or its surroundings, but how much more real and impressive will the story be, if the preacher can present, in a few lifelike touches, a picture of this sacred site, and its environment, as Jesus saw them on that memorable day. In this sketch he might include the twin mountains which rise abruptly from the plain, as if to guard the entrance to the narrow vale between; the wide expanse of the vast grain field which to this day stretches away to the north and south; the sites of Salim, Sychar and Shechem within easy reach; the place of worship to which the woman pointed, on the summit of the sacred mountain of the Samaritans; the dusty road on which the Redeemer travelled, skirting the base of this mountain; and, stranger than all, the stone curb, deeply grooved on its inner face by the water-drawer's rope, recently brought to the light, on which for a few moments the Saviour rested His weary limbs at the midday hour.

It is a significant fact that living fountains of water, easily distinguished from afar by the patches of "green pastures" which surround them, or partly ruined wells, as at Beersheba and the valley of Gerar, have been found at every one of the noted camping-places of the Patriarchs. Not less interesting in this connection, is the fact—vouched for by Colonel Conder and other authorities—that large rock platforms, smoothed and levelled by human hands, presumably as the foundation space for the tabernacle and its courts, have been found at Shiloh, Gibeon and Kirjath-Jearim. In two of these places, according to the sacred record, the tabernacle was pitched as a permanent habitation, while in the third the ark was probably housed in a structure similar to the tabernacle. At Shiloh, the platform, or level court, measures 412 feet in length by 77 in width.

In the history of the Conquest we read with wonder of fenced cities, which seemed to the faint-hearted spies to be " walled up to heaven," but the wonder grows when we study the recent reports of excavations among the low hills on the western slope of Judea; or when we follow Warren, Wilson and Bliss through underground cuttings and tunnels to the substructions of ancient walls, some of which, if they were cleared to their bases to-day, would rise before us to the height of more than 150 feet.

At Tell el Hesy, the mound of many cities, the long lost stronghold of Lachish has been uncovered in part to the lowest level; and there, amid massive brick walls, twenty-eight feet thick, were found Amorite pottery of a distinctive type and many other articles, such as bronze weapons and tools, having the undoubted characteristics of a Pre-Israelite age. More wonderful still was the finding in this ancient mound of a clay tablet in the cuneiform language addressed to Zimrida, Governor of Lachish, from Egypt. This is the counterpart of the famous letters found at Tell Amarna, in Egypt, in the year 1888, from Zimrida to the reigning Pharaoh, whose servant or vassal he acknowledges himself to be.

During the last quarter of the nineteenth century much light had been thrown upon the vexed problems relating to the name, extent and antiquity of the city of Jerusalem.

Some writers have spoken of it as "the sleepy little city of the Jebusites": "the little capital of a petty Highland chief," etc., while others have denied its existence prior to the Exodus, or have refused to admit that it was identical with the Salem of Genesis or the Book of Psalms.

We now know from the long-buried tablets, which were found at Tell Amarna in 1888, that the oldest name of the city was not Jebus, as was generally supposed, but Salem or Uru-Salem—the City of Salem—as the Biblical record asserts (Gen. 14:18; Ps. 76:2; Josh. 18:28; 1 Chron. 11:4).

Five or six of the Tell Amarna tablets were written by the king of Jerusalem to the reigning Pharaoh more than a century before the Exodus; and they witness not only to the antiquity of the city, but to its importance as a royal and priestly city, the ruler of which had a recognized place of influence and power, at that time, in the land.

It is worthy of note in this connection that Professor Sayce has found the same name, Salem, in a slightly different form, among the name-lists in the Egyptian records of the conquest of Canaan.

As to the extent of the city in later times the late Honorary Secretary of the Palestine Exploration Fund, Walter Besant, has this to say:

"Our researches have restored the splendors of the Holy City. We have proved how the vast walls of the Temple—the grandest enclosure of the finest building in the whole world—rose from deep valleys on three sides, presenting a long façade of wall crowned with pillars and porticoes, and how within them rose the gleaming white marbles of the Inner House with its courts and its altars, and its crowd of priests, and those who lived by the altar.

"Our researches have shown the inner valley bridged by noble arches and pierced by subterranean passages.

"They have shown the city provided with a magnificent water supply, glorious with its palaces, its gardens, its citadel, its castle, its courts, and its villas.

"It is a great town that we have restored; not a commercial town, but a great religious centre, to which, at the Passover season, more than 2,000,000 people brought their offerings."

The close correspondences which have been shown in the instances already presented are only samples of a long list of similar illustrations. "There are," says Colonel Conder, "more than 840 places noticed in the Bible which were either in Palestine or the desert of Beersheba and Sinai, and of these nearly three-quarters have now been discovered and marked on maps. Omitting those which may in any sense be doubtful—and these for the most part are unimportant or have bare mention in the record—it cannot be said of one that remains that its local features are out of harmony with the history connected with it name."

In this rapid summary attention has been directed to a few of the most important results of recent research within the limits of the Holy Land. In view of these facts the importance of this study as an aid to the study of the Bible cannot be too strongly emphasized. The minister of the gospel or the Sabbath-school teacher might go far afield in any other department of study before he would find such helpful suggestion, such interesting confirmations of the historic statements of the Bible, and such a wealth of information and illustration of the Scripture text.

Introduction 25

To study this Land in its relation to the Book, whose pages are everywhere stamped with its characteristic features, is to live and move amid its hallowed memories, and to feel the uplift and inspiration of its ever-present, sublime realities.

I

HEBRON,—THE RESTING-PLACE OF THE PATRIARCHS

THREE of the sacred cities of Palestine,—Jerusalem, Bethlehem and Hebron—are on the main ridge, or plateau, of the "Hill Country" of Judea.

Hebron, the farthest to the south, is less than twenty miles from Jerusalem and is connected with it by a good carriage road, recently extended from Bethlehem. This road follows the line of the ancient highway over which the Patriarchs travelled to the "Southland"; and at several points broken sections of the old Roman road have also been found.

The location of Hebron seems to have been originally determined by the beauty and fertility of its immediate surroundings, rather than its availability for security or defense. A careful examination of the ground by recent explorers has confirmed the impression that the modern city, which lies in a narrow, upland valley descending from the northwest, covers, for the most part, the site of the city as it existed in the days of Abraham and Joshua.

There are substructions, and ancient ruins above ground, to the northwest, indicating an extension at one time beyond the present limits, but the main part of the town must always have been in the vicinity of the Haram and the great pools on which it depended for its water supply.

While occupying this exceptional position,—under a hill rather than on it—Hebron is nevertheless the highest city above sea level south of the Esdraelon plain in Western Palestine. Its altitude—3,029 feet—is nearly 600 feet above the summit of Mount Moriah, and more than 4,000 feet above the level of the Dead Sea. At this elevation the land of Judah yields the best of its harvests and the richest of its fruitage. To the traveller who has reached this place, in the springtime, by way of the desert, or over the long, arid ridges which lie to the north or the south, the environs of Hebron present a picture of rare beauty and attractiveness. The long, narrow valley in which the city has nestled for so many centuries is a well watered tract. Its green pastures and luxuriant gardens cover every unoccupied point of its surface and extend for some distance up the slopes of the hills which environ it. On the terraced hillsides above this green basin there are picturesque groupings of fruit trees,—fig, apricot, pomegranate, almond and olive—with here and there a thickly-set vineyard, surrounded by massive stone walls.

The Vale of Mamre, which opens out to the northwest, has long been famous for the choice products of its vineyards and oliveyards. Here vineyard joins to vineyard, and every foot of ground is carefully cultivated. Nowhere in all

HEBRON AND ITS ENVIRONS.

The great Mosque which covers the site of the cave of Machelah is a conspicuous object in the background of the picture.

the land at the present time are the vineyards so numerous and extensive. The vine-stalks, which are usually cut off five or six feet from the ground and supported at the end by forked sticks, at an angle of about thirty degrees, are as stout as the vines which grow in our green houses and conservatories, and the clusters of grapes which they support are exceptionally large and luscious.

Among the vineyards at the northern end of the valley, something more than a mile from Hebron, there is a famous tree, known as Abraham's Oak, which is supposed to stand on or near the site of the camping-place of the Patriarch when he received the visit of the angels. It is an evergreen oak, or Sindian, as the natives call it, and is at least two or three centuries old. Its girth, a few inches above the ground, is twenty-three feet, and formerly its branches covered an area of more than ninety feet in diameter. In recent years some of its largest branches have been broken off by the storms, and it has lost the greater part of its leafy crown. This magnificent tree while it has no direct connection with Abraham is a worthy successor of the great oaks,—far more numerous in ancient times than now—which once grew singly or in groves on many a ridge or high place all along the line of the patriarchal highway from Shechem to Hebron.

A very ancient tradition has associated Mamre with the "Vale of Eshcol"; and certainly so far as present indications can aid in the determination of this location there is no place where the products of the vine may be found in larger clusters or richer profusion. There are evidences, however, that extensive vineyards were cultivated long centuries ago in the Negeb, or south country,—now given over to barrenness and desolation—and it is not unlikely that the great cluster, which the spies secured, on the return journey as a specimen of the products of the good land, was taken from some fertile valley in this locality. It is interesting to note that an account of Hebron and its environs, given by an Arab traveller about A. D. 1000 corresponds, at nearly every point, with its present condition. "All the country about Hebron," he says, "for the distance of half a stage, is filled with villages and vineyards, and grounds bearing grapes and apples, and it is even as though it were all but a single orchard of vines and fruit trees. The district goes by the name of Jebel Nusrah. Its equal for beauty does not exist elsewhere, nor can fruits be finer. A great part of them are sent away to Egypt and into all the country around."

Hebron in its structure and general appearance, as well as in its history, is a city of the past. Its residents are bigoted Moslems, who look with distrust upon the introduction of all modern improvements, and strenuously resist the concessions to Western civilization, which have partially transformed other portions of the land. Because of this conservatism in customs and habits of life

ABRAHAM'S OAK IN THE VALE OF MAMRE.
In recent years this noble tree has lost the greater part of its leafy crown.

it has been said with truth that "no city in Palestine so carries one back to earliest patriarchal times." The houses are built of smooth hard limestone and in general are two stories high and closely joined together. Many have domed roofs as in Jerusalem, and other cities of the East. The streets are narrow and dark and the bazars are jumbled together in dingy recesses and tunnel-like closes, where, at times, it is almost impossible to make headway against the jostling crowd.

In the Vale of Hebron there are two great pools or reservoirs which without doubt are of great antiquity. They are strongly built of hewn stone with steps leading down to the water from the four corners. The smaller one, on the western outskirts of Hebron, is eighty-five feet long and fifty-five wide; its depth is about nineteen feet. The larger pool is lower down in the valley at the south side of the city. It is one hundred and thirty-three feet square and twenty-two feet deep. There can scarcely be a doubt that this is "the Pool in Hebron" where David hanged up the hands and feet of the murderers of Ish-bosheth. The carefully squared stones which surround this gleaming water-mirror in the green valley were put in place long before the foundations of Athens or Rome were laid: and yet this relic of the past upon which David looked in his youthful days, is modern in comparison with the rock-hewn sepulchre of the patriarchs, on the east side of the valley. This hallowed site, the most authentic and interesting of all the ancient burial places on earth, has been carefully guarded from intrusion for many centuries, by the high walls of the Haram, or sanctuary, which enclose it; and the forbidden ground within the precincts of the great mosque, which covers it. This massive structure, with its minarets, buttresses and surrounding walls, occupies the highest part of the town and looms up conspicuously above all other objects within the limits of the valley.

The Haram wall, according to the measurements given by Dr. Robinson, is 200 feet in length, 150 in breadth and 60 feet in height. It is built of large, drafted, smoothly-hewn stones, which in style and dressing resemble the great stones in the foundation of the wall of the Temple area in Jerusalem. One of these stones is thirty-eight feet long and three or four feet in depth. There are sixteen square pilasters, without capitals or well-defined cornices, on each side and eight on the ends. "These pilasters," says Dr. Thomson, "are a feature quite unique, and mark it off from any other edifice I have examined."

The position which the Haram occupies necessitated the cutting away of the rocks on the upper side in order to secure space for the foundation walls. In other words the building was fitted into the hillside; and hence the rock within, —as Dr. Henderson suggests—must be an isolated knoll. As it originally appeared, however, the entrance to the tomb was in the face of the low cliff, or ledge, which extends for some distance along the hillside.

In the Memoirs of the Survey Party (Vol. III, p. 346) the writer says,—"It would almost seem as if the Hebron Haram were a copy in miniature of the Temple enclosures at Jerusalem." This similarity to which Dr. Robinson directed attention nearly sixty years ago, is more strongly marked in the *older* portion of the wall of the Temple area than in that which Warren and others regard as an *addition*, dating from the reign of Herod. This fact seems to be overlooked by Colonel Conder and some of the later authorities, who maintain that the Hebron Haram is the work of the Herodian period. It is a significant fact, also, that there is no evidence, furnished by history or tradition, which connects Herod the Great or any of his successors with this great work. On the contrary it is implied by Josephus in the "history of the Jewish Wars" that costly buildings, noted for their admirable construction, were on this site before his time; and in the "Antiquities" (I, XIV) he tells us that "both Abraham and his descendants built themselves sepulchres, or monuments, in that place." However this may be it is scarcely possible that the descendants of Abraham, who held this sacred burial-place as a possession for a stretch of nearly fifteen centuries, should leave it to be unmarked or unguarded from generation to generation.

A summary of the argument in support of an earlier date than that of Herod is admirably given by Dean Stanley in his "History of the Jewish Church" (Vol. I, p. 482). In concluding he says, "The walls, as they now stand, and as Josephus speaks of them, must have been built before his time. The terms which he uses imply this; and he omits to mention them amongst the works of Herod the Great, the only potentate who could or would have built them in his time, and amongst whose buildings they must have occupied, if at all, a distinguished place. But, if not erected by Herod, there is then no period at which we can stop short of the monarchy. So elaborate and costly a structure is inconceivable in the disturbed and impoverished state of the nation after the return. It is to the kings, at least, that the walls must be referred, and, if so, to none so likely as one of the sovereigns to whom they are ascribed by Jewish and Mussulman tradition, David or Solomon. Beyond this we can hardly expect to find a continuous proof."

The only opening from the outside in the Haram wall is the grand portal through which the Moslem worshippers enter the mosque.

This door was broken through the wall by order of one of the Caliphs in the tenth century. It is probable that the original entrance to the enclosure, prior to the erection of the Moslem addition, now known as Joseph's tomb, was in the northeast corner. Canon Dalton, a competent authority on this point, asserts that there are no traces of an entrance visible in the exterior walls anywhere else: and as this is the only place where the Moslem additions cover up the walls to any extent, he concludes that the original entrance, in Herodian and Byzantine times, must now be covered by this erection.

The Cave of Machpelah is in the southern end of the enclosure, and the massive building which covers it occupies about one third of the Haram area. This building was originally a Christian Church, and, as its construction indicates, was partly Byzantine and partly mediæval. When it fell into the hands of the Moslems, in the year 1187, it was converted into a mosque. For more than seven centuries the entrance to this mosque has been sacredly guarded by a hereditary succession of Moslem rulers, known as the "guardians of the mosque."

At the present time this guard of honor numbers forty, and they are comfortably housed in buildings adjacent to the Haram. Two or three travellers, who did not profess the Moslem faith, claim to have entered the mosque, by special favor or in disguise, prior to the middle of the nineteenth century, but these claims have not been established by satisfactory evidence. In modern times the first representatives of the Christian faith who were permitted to enter this long guarded shrine, were the Prince of Wales—now Edward VII of England—and his party in the year 1862. Dean Stanley, who was one of this distinguished company, has given a careful description of the interior of the building, and this account has been supplemented by the narrative of others who have been accorded the like privilege at later dates. These persons are the Marquis of Bute and party, who entered the mosque in 1866; the Crown Prince of Prussia—the late Emperor Frederick III of Germany—in 1869; the Princes Albert and George, sons of the Prince of Wales, accompanied by Sir Charles Wilson and Colonel Conder, in April, 1882; and General Lew Wallace and Dr. Selah Merrill, with a small party of friends in November of the same year (1882).

The obstacles thrown in the way of the visit of the Prince of Wales were almost insuperable, but wise diplomacy and the incentives of political interests at length prevailed. It is said that when the royal party came to the chapel dedicated to Abraham, the guardians groaned aloud, while their chief with evident agitation, exclaimed: "The Princes of any other nation should have passed over my dead body sooner than enter. But to the eldest son of the Queen of England, we are willing to accord this privilege."

"Once within the mosque," says Dr. Merrill, "my feelings were those of disappointment,—first, at its size. It is not large or imposing. This may be due partly to the fact that the space is divided into different rooms. Secondly I was disappointed to find it in such a neglected condition. The ornamentation on the walls had fallen here and there, and the general air was one of dilapidation and decay. On the other hand the floor of the mosque was covered with some of the most elegant Turkish rugs that I have ever seen."

The same writer describes the position and characteristics of the monumental tombs as follows:—"The Mediæval church at the southern end of the building contains the tombs of Isaac and Rebekah. In the porch on the right hand as one enters the church is the tomb of Abraham, and on the left that of Sarah. Across the open court, and in the northern end of the building, are the tombs of Jacob and Leah, while that of Joseph is in an adjoining apartment, as if it were an afterthought to the original group. These six tombs, not counting that of Joseph, are arranged on the floor of the mosque at equal distances from each other. They are in reality only cenotaphs eight feet long, four feet wide and six feet high, all being about the same size and shape, and having rounded tops. They are covered with costly pieces of silk, embroidered with gold, those on the men's tombs being green and those on the women's bright rose color—the gifts of Sultans or other worldly and powerful defenders of the Moslem faith. Each cenotaph stands in a separate enclosure or room, the entrance to which is guarded by a railing or gate. Those belonging to the tombs of Abraham and Sarah were said to be of silver; but where the silver had been worn away we saw that the gates were really made of iron." This description makes it plain that the cenotaphs or monuments on the floor of the mosque do not indicate the relative position of the bodies in the cave, or crypt below, as some writers have asserted. They only represent the real tombs in the rock-hewn cave, the entrance to which has long been closed to Moslems as well as to the adherents of the Jewish and Christian faiths, and their position was evidently determined by the internal arrangements of the building and the convenience of the worshippers.

The most interesting thing which has been described in connection with the Mediæval church is a round hole in the floor, a few steps south of the cenotaph of Abraham. This opening pierces the roof of a square chamber, which appears to be the vestibule, or outer court, of the Cave of Machpelah. This chamber is lighted by a silver lamp, suspended by a chain from the mouth of the opening. Looking down into the chamber, with the lamp lowered to the floor, Colonel Conder saw a small square door in its south wall. This he describes, as just like the doors of rock-cut tombs all through Palestine.

This aperture, too small for the entrance of a human body, is the only visible connection or opening, so far as known at the present time, with the Cave of Machpelah of the patriarchs. Down this hole the Moslems drop their written prayers, but a superstitious dread of fatal consequences restrains them from entering the precincts of this sacred burial-place, and there is no reliable evidence that any one has entered it within the last six hundred years. "Once, they say, centuries ago, the servant of a great King entered the cave, but returned blind and deaf, wrinkled and crippled." During the period of the Crusades no obstacles were in the way of explorers, and without doubt there was at that time a stairway leading down from the church to the cave. If the vague accounts which have come down to us from that period can be relied upon, the cave, as they saw it, was double, with a vestibule, or entrance room in front. They also make mention of six oblong stone slabs upon which the figures of the patriarchs and their wives were cut in relief. These stone effigies, says Canon Dalton, which are similar to those of the Norman period, would in course of time become covered with a green discoloration and deposit, owing to the dampness of the cave, and hence the patriarchs' bodies are described by those who have seen them since that date to be "clothed in green garments."

The story of the successive burials in this hallowed spot is given us, in language singularly chaste and pathetic, in the solemn charge which Jacob gave to his sons on his deathbed in the land of Egypt—"And he charged them, and said unto them, I am to be gathered unto my people: bury me with my fathers in the cave that is in the field of Machpelah, which is before Mamre, in the land of Canaan, which Abraham bought with the field of Ephron the Hittite for a possession of a burying-place.—There they buried Abraham and Sarah his wife; there they buried Isaac and Rebekah his wife; and there I buried Leah."

In the fulfillment of this sacred obligation Joseph and his brethren reverently carried the embalmed body of Jacob, their father, up to Hebron in the land of Canaan. In this funeral cortège there was a very great company, not of Hebrews only but of Egyptian chariots and horsemen, "with all the servants of Pharoah, the elders of his house, and all the elders of the land of Egypt." The splendor and magnificence of this funeral escort, which, journeying over hill and valley for more than two hundred miles, paused, at length, for the final ceremonies of honor and affection before the entrance of the Cave of Machpelah,—are probably without a parallel in the annals of human history.

Hebron is one of the oldest centres of civilized life in this portion of the ancient world. It is probably as old, if not older, than Damascus, and like this city of the plain it has had a continuous history from the first permanent occupation of the country until the present time. In the book of Numbers the statement is incidentally given that Hebron was built seven years before Zoan, or Tanis, the capital of the shepherd kings in Egypt. "This coupling of Zoan with a Palestinian city," says Mr. Flinders Petrie, "shows that the building must refer to a settlement by Shemites, and not by Egyptians; and considering the age of Hebron it probably refers to the settlement before the eleventh dynasty."

In the course of its long and eventful history Hebron has been in turn the city of the Hittites;

of the Patriarchs; of the Anakim, the much dreaded giant race of the land; of Caleb, the hardy veteran and leader in Joshua's hosts; of the Kohathites, who kept its gates open for a city of refuge; of David, who was crowned in this place and reigned over Judah for "seven years and six months"; of Absalom, the usurper, who raised the standard of rebellion within its walls; of Rehoboam; of the exiles from Babylon; of the Edomites; of the Maccabees; of the Romans; of the Crusaders, and of the Moslems. Among all the shadowy hosts which pass before us in connection with these periods of occupation no single character has left so deep an impression upon this spot as the wandering shepherd from the plains of Chaldea, whose tent was pitched for a time in the "Vale of Mamre before Hebron," and whose only possession in or about the city was the rock-hewn burial-place within its suburbs, which he bought of Ephron, the Hittite.

By the Moslems as well as by the Hebrews and Christians Abraham is acknowledged and revered as the "Father of the Faithful"; and the city which holds his tomb is one of the four sacred cities of the Moslem world.

It is a significant fact also that throughout the Arabic-speaking world the city with which he was so intimately associated has been known, for long ages, as the city of "The Friend." This abbreviated title, in the sense in which the Moslems use it, means the "Friend of Allah":

and is the exact counterpart of the Biblical expression with which we are familiar, —"The Friend of God."

As Dr. Norman Macleod has happily expressed it:—"This is the only spot on earth which attracts to it all who possess the one creed, 'I believe in God.'

"The Holy Sepulchre, in Jerusalem, separates Moslem, Jew, and Christian; here they assemble together. The Moslem guards this place as dear and holy. The Jew from every land draws near to it with reverence and love, and his kisses have left an impress on its stones. Christians of every kindred, and tongue, and creed, visit the spot with a reverence equally affectionate. And who lies here? a great king or conqueror? a man famous for his genius or learning? No; but an old shepherd who pitched his tent 4,000 years ago among these hills, a stranger and a pilgrim in the land, and who was known only as El-Khulil, 'The Friend.' By that blessed name, Abram was known while he lived; by that name he is remembered where he lies buried; and by that name the city is called after him. And it is when all men through faith become with him Friends of God, that all shall be blessed along with 'faithful Abraham.'"

II

BETHLEHEM,—THE BIRTHPLACE OF JESUS

There are two towns in Palestine which have borne the name, Bethlehem, from the days of Joshua until the present time. One is in the territory originally assigned to Zebulun, about seven miles southwest of Nazareth; the other is in the hill country of Judah, a little more than five miles south of Jerusalem. The northern town is mentioned in connection with the allotment of the tribes under Joshua, and again in the book of Judges as the home of Ibzan, the successor of the warrior-judge Jephthah (Josh. 19: 15 ; Judges 12: 8–10).

The original designation of the town in Judah was Ephrath. It had this name in the days of the patriarchs—a term indicative of its fruitful surroundings—but after the conquest it was known as Beth-lehem, the house of bread. In the earlier period of Jewish history it was usually distinguished from Bethlehem in Zebulun by the double name Bethlehem-Judah, or Bethlehem-Ephratah.

For many centuries the ancient city of Zebulun has been in ruins, and its existence has been almost forgotten; while Bethlehem-Ephratah, once among the least of the cities of Judah has become the chief of all the hallowed places of the Land, and its name to-day is one of the most familiar household words throughout the wide domain of Christendom. Bethlehem is on the line of one of the most ancient caravan routes from Syria to Egypt, and, like Bethel, Jerusalem and Hebron, its suburbs extend eastward almost to the border of the Wilderness of Judea. A few years ago this roadway was graded and made wide enough for carriages as far as Hebron. It begins at the Jaffa gate of Jerusalem and follows the valley of Hinnom as far as the southwest corner of the city wall. Thence it continues southward to the entrance of the broad valley or plain of Rephaim, which it traverses for a mile or more until it contracts into a narrow valley and bears off to the west. From this point the route ascends the northern slope of a rocky ridge to the Greek convent of Mar Elyas, which occupies a commanding outlook in a slight depression on its summit. From this elevation the traveller gets his first glimpse of Bethlehem, and here also he can see a portion of the city of Jerusalem. From Mar Elyas the road descends to Rachel's Tomb where it diverges slightly from the main route and leads by a gradual ascent to the gate of the city.

Bethlehem crowns the summit of a long, chalky ridge which projects eastward from the main range. On the north, east and west where the ridge stands clear of the plateau the slopes, naturally abrupt, have been fashioned by the hand of man into irregular groupings of broad

BETHLEHEM OF JUDEA.

terraces, rising in places like giant stairways to the summit.

These terraces are supported by retaining walls of large stone blocks and within these stone ramparts the rich alluvial soil carried up from the valleys nourishes acres of vineyards and olive yards, with here and there a grove or orchard of flourishing fig and almond-trees. Nowhere in all the hill country of Judah do we find a succession of terraced slopes in a state of better preservation, and nowhere can we get a better impression of the advantages of this ancient method of cultivation, by which, in the good days of Israel's prosperity, the hills now barren and waste yielded rich harvests of grass and grain as well as the choicest fruits of the olive, the fig, and the vine.

As seen from the northern and eastern approaches the terraced heights, which sweep in graceful curves around the shoulder of the hill, the long line of white houses, which seem to rise in tiers above them, the steep ascent to the gate, and the pile of massive fortress-like buildings, which surround the Church of the Nativity—present a picture of rare beauty and attractiveness. While nominally a Christian village, Bethlehem retains more of the ancient Jewish types of village life and architecture than any other town of Southern Palestine. In its solidly constructed stone houses, with central courts; its flat roofs; its latticed windows and its narrow streets, flanked by blank walls on either hand;

we see far more of the ancient than of the mediæval or the modern. Says Canon Tristram, "This chalky ridge crowned with the long narrow street, with various alleys on either side of it, presents us with one of the few remaining specimens of an old Jewish city, for, excepting in the disappearance of the wall, it is probably unchanged in architecture and arrangement from what it was in the days of David." Founded upon the living rock and undisturbed by battles and sieges through most, if not all the ages of its existence Bethlehem has suffered but little from change and decay. Ancient Jerusalem has passed through more than a score of sieges and now lies under ruin heaped upon ruin, but Bethlehem in the midst of the destructions and desolation which have swept over the land of Judah, has ever been a sheltered spot; and, as becometh the birthplace of the Lord of Glory, has remained through all the changeful centuries, a "home of peace,"—a "house of plenty."

> "O little town of Bethlehem
> How still we see thee lie;
> Above thy deep and dreamless sleep
> The silent stars go by."

The first mention of this upland village is in connection with a pathetic incident in the life of Jacob, well nigh forty centuries ago. As the patriarch, after many years of absence in Padan Aram, drew near to this place on his return journey to the home of his childhood in the South country, his beloved wife Rachel was prostrated by a fatal illness. In giving birth to Benjamin her own life went out and she was buried by the wayside. Over her precious remains Jacob erected a pillar, and from that day until the present time the spot where Rachel sleeps has never remained without some mark to preserve its identity. It was a well known place in the days of Moses, and of Samuel and through all the centuries following it has been revered and carefully guarded by Hebrew, Moslem and Christian. When on his deathbed in Egypt, many years after the death of Rachel, Jacob made mention of this sad bereavement in words of touching tenderness:—"And as for me when I came from Padan, Rachel died by me in the land of Canaan in the way, when there was but a little way to come unto Ephrath: and I buried her there in the way of Ephrath; the same is Bethlehem."

"We may well recall," says a recent writer, "how the prophet represents Rachel sitting weeping for her children as the long train of captive exiles passed from the south on their way to Babylon, and note how the tomb is close to the roadside: and then as we see Bethlehem not a mile distant we understand how aptly the evangelist transfers the figure to the Massacre of the Innocents by Herod."

Some of the most interesting and important events in the providential unfolding of the plan of Redemption are interwoven with the story of Bethlehem. By a Divine allotment and ordination this mountain hamlet of Judah became the ancestral abode of Boaz; the home by choice and adoption of Ruth the Moabitess; and the birthplace of David, the great-grandson of Boaz and Ruth, to whom is given by common consent, and by Divine sanction, the first place on the list of Israel's noblest and most renowned Kings.

At the foot of the terraced slope directly east of Bethlehem there is an open valley or plain, known as the fields of Bethlehem, where Boaz and his reapers labored, and where Ruth gleaned after them among the sheaves. Beyond this strip of cultivated land, in which each inhabitant of the village has his little plot of ground, indicated as in the olden time by a stone landmark, lies a large tract, which reaches to the edge of the Wilderness. This from time immemorial has been the common pasturage of the shepherds of Bethlehem. On this open space, and at times far down on the slopes of the wilderness below, David, in his youthful days, kept his father's flock.

Somewhere on this ancient pasture land, and well nigh a thousand years after David had been gathered to his fathers, a company of shepherds were keeping watch over their flocks by night, "And, lo, the angel of the Lord came upon them, and the glory of the Lord shone round about them; and they were sore afraid. And the angel said unto them, Fear not: for behold, I bring you good tidings of great joy, which shall be to all people. For unto you is born this day in the city of David a Saviour, which is Christ the Lord. And this shall be a sign unto you; Ye shall find the babe wrapped in swaddling clothes, lying in a manger." When the angel began to speak to this little company on that night of wonders he was alone; but as he ceased there was a rustle in the air, a quivering of swiftly moving wings, a glare of surpassing brightness, "and, suddenly, there was with the angel a multitude of the heavenly host praising God and saying, Glory to God in the highest, and on earth peace, good-will towards men."

"And it came to pass, as the angels were gone away from them into heaven, the shepherds said one to another, Let us go now even unto Bethlehem, and see this thing which is now come to pass, which the Lord hath made known unto us. And they came with haste and found Mary, and Joseph, and the babe lying in a manger."

In these inspired words, so artless in arrangement and so sublime in signification the evangelist tells the story of the announcement of the Holy Birth of the Babe in Bethlehem. There are good grounds for the commonly accepted belief that the Church of the Nativity covers the site of the inn or lodging-place in which this amazing event took place. More than five hundred years before the birth of Christ the prophet Jeremiah makes mention of the "habitation" or caravansary of Chimham, which was by Bethlehem, on the way to Egypt (Jer. 41:17). This was probably a portion of the patrimony of David which was given to Chimham by the king, at whose table he was an honored guest, as a token of gratitude for the kindness shown to him, when an exile in the land of Gilead, by Barzillai, his father (2 Sam. 19: 39, 40; 1 Kings 2: 7). It is scarcely possible that in a town so small as Bethlehem there would have been more than one khan or caravansary; and it is a well known fact that the location of buildings of this character has rarely, if ever, been changed in Eastern countries.

In its ordinary form the khan consists of a square or oblong enclosure or court, constructed of rubble or hewn stone, with chambers of one or two stories built inside or against the inner walls. On one side—usually the side opposite the gate—of this enclosure, there are stalls or stables in which the animals belonging to the caravans or travelling parties can be sheltered and protected. Sometimes the khan is located at the base of a low ridge or cliff, which serves as a wall on one side, and in such cases the stalls or stables are recesses or caves, easily made by burrowing into the face of the soft, limestone rock. "Many inns or khans," says Dr. Thomson, "have caverns of greater or less extent below them—that is on the ground floor,—where cattle and flocks are sheltered, and stone mangers, like those in stables, are built along the walls." In view of these facts there is nothing incredible, in itself, in the tradition which indicates a grotto in the crypt of the Church of the

Nativity as the place where our Lord was born. The stately Basilica, which for fifteen hundred and seventy-four years has marked this hallowed spot, was built by Helena, the mother of Constantine. It is unquestionably the oldest monument of Christian architecture in the world. It escaped destruction when all other houses of Christian worship were destroyed; and for more than fifteen centuries the birth of Christ has been celebrated at Christmastide, with great pomp and ceremony, within its walls. It is a significant fact, also, that the grotto, now known as the "Chapel of the Nativity," was regarded as the birthplace of our Lord two hundred years before the Basilica of Helena was erected. Justin Martyr, who was born about the beginning of the second century—only a few years after the death of the apostle John—describes the place of Christ's birth as "a certain cave close to the village of Bethlehem" (Dial. ii. 7). A century later Origen asserts that the cave in which he was born and the manger in which he was laid were still shown in Bethlehem. Eusebius and Jerome confirm this testimony and the latter gave the best evidence of his belief in the genuineness of the site by taking up his permanent abode in a similar grotto close beside it. Here he lived and labored for the greater part of his long life, giving to the Christian world as the result of his patient labors, in this lowly abode, the Latin or Vulgate version of the Scriptures.

Colonel Conder of the Survey party, who had

exceptional opportunities for the investigation of the evidence which bears upon the authenticity of this site, sums up the testimony in its favor as follows:—" This is almost the only site which we can trace earlier than the time of Constantine, and the tradition seems to me to be credible, because, throughout this part of Palestine, there are innumerable instances of stables cut in rock, resembling the Bethlehem grotto. Such stables I have planned and measured at Tekoa, Aziz, and other places south of Bethlehem, and the mangers existing in them leave no doubt as to their use and character. The credibility of this tradition thus appears to be far greater than that attaching to the later discoveries, by which the enthusiastic Helena and the politic Constantine settled the scenes of other Christian events; and the rude grotto with its rocky manger, may, it seems to me, be accepted even by the most sceptical modern explorers."

The plan of the Church of the Nativity accords very closely with the description given by Eusebius of the original Church of the Holy Sepulchre at Jerusalem, which was also built under the direction of Constantine. It is one hundred and twenty feet in length by one hundred and ten in width. The interior consists of a central nave thirty-four feet wide and two aisles on each side of it twenty-five feet in width. The lateral aisles are separated by a double row of monolithic columns twenty feet high and two and a half feet in diameter. There are eleven of these massive pillars in each row. The floor is paved with large slabs of stone, broken in places and deeply worn by the tread of countless worshippers, most of whom have tarried but a few hours, or days at most, within its sacred precincts. The roof beams of the Church were originally of cedar brought from Lebanon, but during the reign of Edward IV of England these were replaced by beams of English oak. One of the most notable events within the walls of this ancient sanctuary was the coronation of Baldwin as King of Jerusalem, on Christmas Day of the year 1101.

The Chapel or Grotto of the Nativity is under the choir at the east end of the Church. The floor of this rock-hewn chamber, which is reached by a double flight of steps, is paved with marble. Its walls, except at one or two places—where the native rock may be seen—are lined with the same material and decorated with hangings of embroidery in silk and gold. Beneath a recess at the eastern end of the chamber a silver star let into the marble floor glows in the light of sixteen ever-burning silver lamps which hang above it; while around it is the inscription in Latin, which many a traveller from far-away lands has read through tear-dimmed eyes,—"Hic de Virgine Maria Jesus Christus natus est." Whatever we may think of the locality itself, that silver star in Bethlehem commemorates the greatest event in the long history of time. Here Love became incarnate, that Love might suffer and redeem. This Incarnation is the miracle of miracles, more wonderful even than the miracle of the Resurrection. It is now and ever shall be the crowning mystery of godliness that He, the Word, who was with God and who was God; "whose goings forth have been from of old, from everlasting"—"was made flesh" and came to dwell among us.

> "For Christ is born of Mary
> And gathered all above
> While mortals slept, the angels kept
> Their watch of wond'ring love.
> O morning stars! together
> Proclaim the Holy Birth
> And praises sing to God the King
> And peace to men on earth!"

III

NAZARETH,—THE HOME OF JESUS

The place where our Lord was "brought up" is a secluded spot in the southern portion of the highlands of Lower Galilee. It nestles in a mountain-rimmed basin, nine hundred and fifty feet above the Esdraelon plain, and is one and a half miles back of its northern border. It is almost due north of Jerusalem, and is only two miles east of the midway point between the Mediterranean and the Sea of Galilee. Through all the changes of the centuries, Nazareth has retained its ancient name, and the genuiness of the site itself has never been questioned.

The depression in which Nazareth and its outlying fields and gardens are embosomed is formed by the convergence of several valleys, and the drainage from the hills which environ it makes it a basin of more than ordinary fertility. The rim of the circlet of rounded hills,—fifteen in number—which shut it in, is rocky and barren, but the inner slopes on the south and east are well cultivated. Says Canon Tristram, " This encircling cluster of hills is in fact the melting away of the hills of Galilee as they are lost in the plain of Esdraelon. Nazareth clings to the slope of the last of these which deserves the name of hill, while the amphitheatre in front is formed by the smaller ridges, mere gentle swellings enclosing the shallow basin, which forms the foreground in their sweep. Here cornfields mingle with vineyards and fig-trees, and the occasional date palm, which in this valley reach their northern limit, are marked features in the home landscape."

The town, as the modern traveller sees it, lies on the northwestern side of the basin, which is a mile or more in length, and something less than a half mile in breadth. It is now rapidly outgrowing its former limits towards the south, but formerly it occupied a higher position on the hillside. The most attractive portion of the confines of Nazareth is the open space at the lower end of the basin. This is the village green, where fields and gardens separated by stone fences, or hedges of cactus, twelve or fifteen feet high, overspread the levels, and olives and vines thickly dot the higher slopes. At this point the elevation above the sea level is 1,140 feet. The top of the hill on the western side, which rises directly above the town, is 458 feet higher.

The usual way of approach to Nazareth from the south is by a well-beaten road which leads obliquely across the Plain of Esdraelon to a break in the range of the Galilean hills at the mouth of a wady which comes down from the Nazareth basin. From this point a steep and narrow pathway, which horses climb with difficulty, leads up to the southeastern quarter of the city. At

NAZARETH, THE HOME OF JESUS.

the present time several roads lead out from Nazareth to adjacent towns along the great lines of travel. On the eastern side of the basin a good road leads to Tiberias by way of Mount Tabor; to the northeast there is a road to Cana (Kefr Kenna); to the north to Seffurieh, the old Roman capital of Galilee; to the west to Haifa, and to the southwest by way of Yafa to the Esdraelon plain. Some of these roads have been recently constructed and the others have been greatly improved within the past twenty years.

The first view of Nazareth from the ridge which overlooks it on the southeast is singularly beautiful and impressive. The flat-roofed houses are larger and more solidly built than in most of the cities of the east, and the white limestone used in their construction shines in the clear sunlight with dazzling brightness.

The narrow streets, which climb the hill in successive terraces; the outcropping ledges of rock which stand out above the town, and, in some places extend like a great wall along one side of the streets; the natural amphitheatre with its background of bare hills; the fields and gardens, which extend far down the valley; and the larger buildings surrounded by massive stone walls, belonging to the various sects and religious orders of Nazareth,—are some of the most striking features of this distant view. A nearer look dispels some of the illusions which attach to this first view, but it is nevertheless true that the city as a whole is much more attractive and interesting in its appearance and surroundings than any of the Moslem towns of Galilee or Samaria. The largest and most imposing structure in Nazareth is the Latin Monastery. The Church of the Annunciation, the Chapel of St. Joseph, the so-called kitchen of the Virgin Mary, and other convenient traditional sites, of more than doubtful authenticity are included within its high walls.

Near this building the Latins have also a large hospice and orphanage, a nunnery and school for girls. At the other end of the town the Orthodox Greeks have a monastery, a church dedicated to the Angel Gabriel, a college for teachers, a school for boys and girls, and a hospice for the use of pilgrims. On the western side the Maronites have a church, and east of it the United Greeks have a house of worship which they claim occupies the site of the Synagogue of Nazareth. Under Protestant auspices and control there are an English church and Mission, a Bible depot, a Scotch and a German hospital, and high up on the hill above the town an orphanage for girls. The new Serai, or residence of the Moslem Governor, and a mosque, with graceful dome and minaret, occupy a considerable space north of the Latin Convent on the eastern side of the town. On the south side there is a large threshing floor—a typical representative of its kind—which is frequently used as a camping place for tourists. A more desirable spot for this purpose, however, is an open space among the orchards of figs and olives in the vicinity of the Greek Church of the Annunciation.

While the natural landmarks in and about Nazareth remain unchanged there is but little in the town itself which we can confidently associate with our Lord, or the times, in which He lived. There are no traces of gates or surrounding walls, or of the ruins of public buildings of any sort: and there is not a house standing to-day which can be identified with any building upon which His eyes rested when He was here among men. The place, as it now appears, is without doubt the successor of the place whose name it still bears, but it is a modern city in everything perhaps, except its streets, which are truly Oriental in their narrowness, their untidy appearance, their apparently aimless windings, and in the unique fashion of their paving.

The so-called "holy places" which tradition has localized here are all apocryphal, and have no claim to veneration or regard. The intelligent visitor does not come to Nazareth to see holy places but a holy place. It is a place forever memorable and sacred not because of one or more conspicuous events, but because it was the home of Jesus for nearly thirty years of His earthly life. Here the Holy One of God dwelt among men, and every foot of this little mountain-rimmed basin has been hallowed by His steps.

Among the natural features of the place, which we have every reason to believe have come down through all the Christian centuries without appreciable change, three are specially noteworthy.

One is the line of cliffs which rise behind the Maronite church; another is the public fountain, known as Mary's Well; and the third is the rounded crest of the hill upon which the greater part of the city is built.

(1) The cliffs in the position indicated are partially hidden by rubbish and a luxuriant growth of cactus and thorny shrubs, but a careful examination has disclosed two or three precipitous walls of rock thirty or forty feet in height. "One of them," says Dr. Manning, "had a considerable accumulation of débris at the bottom, which, if cleared away, would probably give twenty feet more." This wall of rock overhanging the modern town suggested to Dean Stanley the possibility that "the brow of the hill on which the city was built," where the Saviour's life was threatened by those who had listened to Him in the Synagogue (Luke 4: 29), was not beneath the town, where tradition has located it, but over it and on its upper edge, if not included within its limits. The only ruins of ancient buildings which have been found are on the platform above the cliff, and Colonel Conder thinks it possible that the synagogue may have stood upon this elevation.

From these indications it has been inferred, also, that the ancient town was higher up the slope than the houses now extend.

(2) The Fountain of Nazareth is in the midst of the gardens at the eastern edge of the town. Its spring-head is in the crypt of the Church of

the Angel Gabriel—the Greek Church of the Annunciation. The water issues from the rock in a full, clear stream from the north side of the crypt, and is conducted past the altar to a well or cistern let down into the pavement, from which the water is dipped up by attendants for the use of the Greek pilgrims. The church occupies the site of an older structure which existed in the time of Arculph, A. D. 700. A conduit, partly rock-hewn and partly of masonry, which bears the marks of great antiquity conveys the water from the church to an open space near by, whence it issues under a vaulted arch in several streams for the convenience of the water carriers.

The surplus water, which frequently overflows the stone tank provided for it and forms a little pool around it, is used to irrigate the gardens. The place of the fountain is the most heartsome spot in or about the city, and were it not for the fact that it has always been a place of public resort, we might accept the site selected by the Greek inventors of sacred places as the most likely one for the scene of the Annunciation. The fountain itself has been from time immemorial the one source of fresh water supply for the inhabitants of Nazareth. It is the centre of social life where the shepherds come to water their flocks; where the pilgrim stops to quench his thirst; and where women and maidens in picturesque attire congregate in the cool of the day to gossip about neighborhood affairs, and to fill their earthern pitchers, as they have done for centuries;—as they did without doubt in Mary's day. "Often and often," says Canon Tristram, "may the infant Saviour have passed to this spot with His mother, as the boys do now, following her.

"The path under the olive-trees, like that from Bethany round the base of Olivet and like Jacob's Well, is one of the few where we may be perfectly sure we are treading for the moment in His earthly footsteps."

(3) The crest of the hill which rises above the city on its western side, known as Jebel es Sikh, is the highest point in the circlet of mountains which hide the vale of Nazareth from the outside world. The outlook from its rounded summit, where stands the Wely of Neby Isma'l, commands one of the grandest and most distinctly outlined panoramic views in Palestine. The mountains of Naphtali, the snowy dome of Mt. Hermon, the deep depression of the Jordan valley, the highlands of Bashan and Gilead, Tabor and Little Hermon, and Gilboa, the great plain of Esdraelon, and the historic towns that border it, the high mountains of Ephraim, the long ridge of Mt. Carmel, and a vast stretch of the blue waters of the Mediterranean Sea,—are all included in the sweep of vision—covering thirty miles in three directions—from the summit of this commanding eminence. This is the only place, as Dean Stanley intimates, where the three sacred mountains, Tabor, Hermon and Carmel are conjoined in one view. Here our Lord must

often have come to hold communion with the Father; to drink in the fresh breezes from the sea; and to look over the land where His labors and sufferings were to be undertaken for a sinful race.

Looking northward from this view-point over the billowy waves of mountain ridges which stretch onward to the higher ranges of upper Galilee one may trace along the lines of the intervening cross valleys and plains as on a relief map the direction of many an ancient thoroughfare between the sea coast and important towns by the Lake of Galilee or beyond it into the region of the East. One of these great thoroughfares, and the nearest to Nazareth, followed a long, cross valley from Acre, or Ptolemais as it was called in the Roman period, to Sepphoris and Cana, and thence to the plateau above Tiberias, where diverging lines led to the coast towns of the Galilean lake and to Gilead and the Decapolis.

This was one of the chief branches, if not the trunk line itself, of the famous *Via Maris*. Its nearest point to Nazareth was Sepphoris, the Roman capital of the district of Galilee, some four or five miles away. Along this great thoroughfare of The Nations, which Dr. G. A. Smith describes as in sight of the village boys who climbed to the northern edge of their hollow home, "legions marched and princes swept with their retinues, and all sorts of travellers from all countries went to and fro."

From the foot of Mt. Tabor, six miles away, another great thoroughfare, which in ancient times diverged from the Via Maris on the western coast of the Sea of Galilee, may be distinctly traced in its oblique course across the Great Plain to the pass of Megiddo on its southern border. This was the Great South Road from Damascus to Egypt.

Equally distinct in its course, as seen from this outlook, is the Caravan Route which traverses the length of the plain from Bethshan to Haifa at the foot of Mt. Carmel. This was the "Great Road of the East," over which unnumbered hosts have travelled year by year and century by century since the days of the patriarchs. "Up it," says Dr. Smith, "have come through all ages the Midianites, the children of the east, and in the Roman period it connected the Asian frontier of the Empire with the capital."

It is evident from this vision of the hilltop that the *district* in which our Lord passed the years of His childhood and youth was not buried in obscurity, nor remote from the great centres of life and activity, and progressive civilization. It is indeed true that "the Galilee of the time of Jesus was not only of the richest fertility, cultivated to the utmost, and thickly covered with populous towns and villages, but the centre of every known industry, and the busy road of the world's commerce."

All this, and more, that might be affirmed with

truth of the district as a whole, is not inconsistent with the fact that the early home of Jesus was in a secluded spot above the busy marts of trade, and apart from the moving throng on the highways which traversed the plains.

The near look from this elevation shows us a deep-lying valley among the hills with an unwalled town clinging to its lower slopes, "attractive in its white dress with edgings of green," but hidden and separated by all its *immediate* surroundings. It is literally true that when one stands within it nothing is visible except the hills which shut it in. "No great road led up to this sunny nook" before it became famous as a "Holy Place," and the long processions of trade, war, pleasure, adventure and pomp, which might be seen afar from the hilltop above it, passed it by. The nearest point to any of the great roads to which reference has been made was about five miles, and the routes which led out to them, except, perhaps, the roads to Mt. Tabor and Cana, were probably nothing more than mountain trails. There is no evidence, at least, that the two steep and rugged pathways that led down to the Plain of Esdraelon were ever in better condition than they are today.

In recent years such eminent authorities as Drs. Edersheim and Selah Merrill have challenged the oft-repeated statements that Nazareth was a secluded and obscure village in the period of the Roman occupation, but the evidence upon which their contention is based is too vague and unsatisfactory to affect the generally accepted belief, which has been confirmed by the results of recent research, as well as by the almost unanimous consent of scores of able writers and explorers who have preceded them.

In his great work, the life of Christ, Edersheim accepts the statement of Neubauer that Nazareth was one of the "Priest centres," where those whose duty it was to minister in course at the Temple were accustomed to gather, in order that they might go up in company to Jerusalem, while those who were not appointed for this duty remained in the synagogue to pray. On the assumption that this assertion was grounded upon sufficient evidence the inference might be drawn that the home of Jesus was a well-known ecclesiastical centre, and that there was "a living connection between it and the Temple," but the statement itself rests upon such doubtful rabbinical authority that it is practically worthless as an item of proof. In the same connection Dr. Edersheim claims for Nazareth a position of prominence among the towns of Galilee because it was on the line of the Via Maris, the great thoroughfare, already described, from Acre to Damascus and the cities of the east. In view of the facts already given, with respect to the location and topography of Nazareth there seems to be no valid evidence upon which to base this claim. It does not accord with the course of this great highway as traced by Dr. Smith and other eminent authorities and it is not at all likely that Roman engineers would make such a detour over the mountains from the general direction of the route when they had the long valley before them in which the Roman capital of Galilee was situated. Looking at the place from his own view-point Colonel Conder of the Survey party makes the assertion that "no highroad of trade passed through the village, and the water of a single spring supplied the place, which had no special advantages of soil or water to make it an important centre." Elsewhere he says, "It was, geographically, a place of little note, an obscure, remote hamlet in the mountains, where the childhood of Jesus must have passed without contact with the busier world of trade and political strife."

Dr. Merrill rests his objection to this view mainly upon the proximity of Nazareth to the Roman capital and other important towns: and upon the fact that it is always called a city (polis) in the New Testament. With respect to the first point there is no contention. Its admission, as we have seen, is not inconsistent with the seclusion of a mountain town whose nearest point on any great highway of travel, according to the statement of Dr. Merrill, was measured by an hour and a half of ordinary travel. In regard to the second point it is sufficient to say that the same word (polis) is also used by New Testament writers in describing Bethlehem which at no time in its history, until recent events have brought it into prominence, was anything but a mountain village.

Nazareth is not mentioned among the Old Testament towns, and Josephus, who speaks of important places in its vicinity makes no allusion to it in any of his works. The manner in which the evangelists refer to it, the implied reproach associated with the name by the enemies of Christ, and the fact that no trace of walls or gates or ruins of public buildings have been found in it, point to the conclusion that it was in the time of Christ a quiet rural town, the homestead of shepherds, craftsmen, vine-dressers, and tillers of the soil. It is its "air of quiet, peaceful seclusion," as one has happily expressed it, "that constitutes its chief charm, and its peculiar adaptation to the early history of our Lord."

The first mention of Nazareth by Christian writers, after the days of the evangelists, is in the Onomasticon, where Eusebius describes it as a village not far from Mount Tabor. It does not appear to have been visited, as a holy place, by pilgrims until the sixth century. In the earlier period of the Crusades it was under the control of the Latin Christians, but at a later date it became the seat of a Greek Bishopric, and since that time the Greek influence has been dominant.

In 1837 the town was partly destroyed by an earthquake. Most of the houses have been rebuilt since that date, and a larger number of new ones have been added in recent years, giving to the place a decidedly modern look. Within the past decade especially Nazareth has increased rapidly in wealth and numbers. So far as local influences are concerned Dr. Thomson is doubtless correct when he asserts that the growth of Nazareth is mainly owing to the inroads of the Arabs from beyond Jordan, which render it unsafe to reside in Beisan and on the plain of Esdraelon. "Many places," he says, "have been deserted, and the inhabitants have retired from the plains to Jenin, Nazareth and farther west towards, the seaboard. Should a strong government drive the Bedawin over the Jordan, and keep them there, the population and importance of Nazareth would decline."

From a village of three or four thousand inhabitants it has now become the chief town of its district, with a resident population of about eleven thousand, of whom fully four-fifths are adherents of the Christian faith.

While for the most part they are very imperfect representatives of the religion they profess they have nevertheless caught something of its spirit and have cast their influence on the side of enlightenment and a more advanced civilization. An international telegraph line, a post-office and a good carriage road from Haifa connect Nazareth with the outside world; and from every quarter of the globe tens of thousands of pilgrims visit it every year.

To meet the growing demand for transportation to this early home of Jesus, the largest passenger steamers of the Mediterranean service now touch regularly, during the pilgrimage season, at the port of Haifa to land or receive passengers.

It is a notable fact also, that in this year of Grace (1902) the Celtic of the White Star Line,—the largest and finest vessel which now floats the seas,—carried eight hundred tourists to this port, and tarried a sufficient time to allow a satisfactory visit to this and other sacred places among the hills of Galilee.

The influences which are now contributing to the growth of this mountain city, and which are drawing to it the best and most devout of every land, in ever-increasing numbers—are almost wholly traceable to its connection with the Holy Child who grew up here with winsome manners and irreproachable life from infancy to mature manhood. If it were possible to disassociate this place from the silent years which He spent within its confines: if it were possible to eliminate from the fair prospect, which the traveller from far away lands now looks down upon from the rim of this green basin, all the churches and schools and hospitals and orphanages and homes which have been erected here "in His name"—this prosperous town, which, like Bethlehem, the birthplace of our Lord, ranks with the best and most attractive cities of Palestine, would speedily lose its prestige among the Galilean towns and revert to the littleness and obscurity which characterized it before it became the abiding place of the "Word that was made flesh" and dwelt among men. Take away from Nazareth "the name that is above every name," the name that was coupled with it on the cross, and all the highways that centre in it from every side would shrink into narrow bridle paths; the tide of travel which sweeps back and forth through its streets year by year would cease, and the great vessels which now touch at its port would pass silently by.

This can never be, however, and more and more Nazareth will be dear to the Christian heart as the home of Mary, " highly favored and blessed among women," and the place of the hidings of His power, who for our sakes made Himself of no reputation, and took upon Him the form of a servant, and was made in the likeness of men.

" The scene of his earthly life," says Dr. Thomson, "is altogether in harmony with His character. It is 'Holy Ground'; and whatever may or must be said of its inhabitants, ancient or modern, let us remember that the greatest good God ever bestowed upon our world did 'come out of Nazareth.'"

IV

THE WILDERNESS OF JUDEA

In the time of our Lord the Province of Judea included the territory originally allotted to the tribes of Judah, Benjamin and Dan, together with the greater part if not the whole of the heritage of Ephraim. This rugged and singularly diversified tract divides naturally into four longitudinal sections. The scriptural names, characteristic of these divisions, are:—" The Plain"; the "Shephelah," or region of the low hills; the "Hill Country"; and the "Wilderness."

The Wilderness section includes the whole of the eastern slope, or declivity, of the Judean mountains. It is a tract more than fifty miles in length. Its average width is nine or ten miles. The term Jeshimon, meaning the "Waste" or "Desolation," applies more properly to the portion which borders the Dead Sea, but the same characteristic features prevail all along the eastern slope of the mountains, from the rock fortress of Masada to the northern limit of the territory of Benjamin. It is not a desert in the ordinary acceptation of the term, but a waste or wilderness —as its Old and New Testament names imply— incapable of cultivation except in a few favored spots. From time immemorial it has been "a

DRY BED OF WATERFALL IN WADY DABR.
Wilderness of Judea.

land not inhabited"; a land given over to wild beasts, to hermits and nomads, and to outlaws in hiding. The most rugged and desolate portion borders the Dead Sea where a wall of towering cliffs, cleft at irregular intervals by deep ravines and gorges, rises abruptly to heights varying from twelve to two thousand feet. The variation in levels from the edge of the plateau to the surface of the Dead Sea is but little short of four thousand feet. From the summit of the "hill country" to a depth of two thousand feet the descent may be characterized as a rugged, irregular slope. From the foot of this incline—a level which corresponds with the plane of the Mediterranean Sea—the descent, along the whole line, is steep and precipitous.

The almost innumerable wadies and ravines which cut their way through this district, and break up its surface into an irregular succession of clefts and ridges and shelving beds of earth and rock, are shorter and more direct in their downward course than the water ways on the western side of the range. Near the watershed they are shallow, rock-strewn grooves, but at lower levels they converge into narrow channels, which deepen as they descend into wild gorges, some of which might readily suggest to the poetic fancy of a David or a Job "the valley of the shadow of death." These torrent beds are conduits for the rapid transmission of the floods which come with the bursting of the clouds in the time of the early and the later rains, but in the summer season—except in the lowest beds of the deepest ravines—they are as dry and barren as the broken and crumpled slopes of the ridges that lie between them.

The wildest and deepest of these mountain defiles is the Wady Kelt which enters the Jordan plain near the site of the ancient city of Jericho. It is formed by the convergence of several torrent beds, one of which is the Wady Suweinet. This line of natural cleavage was the route of Joshua's army of invasion, the objective point being Ai at the head of the valley. In the Wady Suweinet, a few miles below the site of Ai, is the celebrated pass of Michmash, the scene of Jonathan's exploit in the days when the hosts of the Philistines overran this portion of the land, and held the approaches to the strongholds of Judah and Benjamin. At this point the valley contracts into a narrow gorge, or canon, eight hundred feet deep, with a sharp projecting rock on one side, facing a similar projection on the other side.

Another notable defile which affords a continuous passageway to the summit of the plateau is the Wady en Nar down which the Kidron flows to the Dead Sea. In its lower stretches this "Valley of Fire," as the name indicates, is shut in by towering cliffs hundreds of feet in height. Into this deep and awful chasm, opening directly to the east, the unclouded rays of the summer's sun shine down, through the morning and midday hours, with dazzling glare and almost torrid heat.

This is the valley of Ezekiel's vision of the healing waters. From his view-point at the outer gate of the Temple—"by the way that looketh eastward"—the prophet beheld the course of the mystic river, which issued from a hidden source beneath the sanctuary and flowed down to the lower levels of the desert plain, in ever-increasing depth and volume. To the resident of the East, where the introduction of a stream of living water brings life, beauty and abundance, causing the wilderness to rejoice and blossom as the rose, no figure could more aptly symbolize the progress and transforming power of the gospel in the coming days of the long promised Messiah.

The Greek Convent of Mar Saba, which clings like a swallow's nest to the face of a towering cliff on one side of the Kidron Valley, is the only human habitation of permanent character within the limits of this desert region. At this point—the wildest and dreariest in the heart of the Wilderness—the precipitous walls of the valley rise to the height of nearly five hundred feet. The chasm between, which resembles a huge railroad cutting, is six hundred feet wide.

Mar Saba is one of the most unique structures of its kind in the world. It was probably a cave-dwelling in the face of the rock at first, and afterwards, as the necessity for enlargement or defense arose, strongly buttressed terraces were made upon which buildings of various kinds were constructed and a massive enclosing wall was laboriously built up from the base of the cliff to its very summit. One outlook from the summit of this wall is said to be 590 feet above the bed of the Kidron Valley. The original structure dates from the fifth century and it has been occupied by an unbroken succession of monks of the Greek church—except when they were driven away by force—from that period until now. At the present time the face of the cliff is almost hidden from view by the walls, towers, buttresses, terraces, chambers, balconies, chapels and shrines which together make up this strange labyrinth of "Kidron's storied dell," in which the natural and the artificial, the grotesque and the sacred are so curiously interblended.

In attestation of the perils to which the anchorites of former days were exposed, the monks of Mar Saba show, behind a grating of iron bars, a gruesome collection of skulls and bones, which are said to represent the remains of 14,000 martyrs, put to death by the Persians in the beginning of the seventh century.

In this dreary solitude, something more than eleven centuries ago, St. Stephen, the Sabaite, wrote the touching words of the antiphonal hymn, which in our English version begins with the familiar words:—

> "Art thou weary, art thou languid
> Art thou sore distressed?
> Come to me, saith One, and coming
> Be at rest."

THE GREEK CONVENT OF MAR SABA.
Wilderness of Judea.

This sweet lyric, translated or rather paraphrased by Dr. Neale, is as evangelical and pure in sentiment and tone as the hymns of Toplady and Charles Wesley. Like the melodious chimes which peal out at eventide from the old belfry of Mar Saba, this hymn of the desert, and the dark ages, has gladdened the heart of many a pilgrim on the wilderness journey to the better land, who, "weary and languid," has been ready to faint or give way to despair.

South of the valley of the Kidron there are possibly a score or more of deep gorges in the mountain wall which borders the Dead Sea, but they do not afford continuous passageways, like the Wady en Nar or the Wady Kelt, to the summit of the plateau. A noteworthy cleft of this group is the pass which leads down to Engedi from the cliff of Ziz, by which the hosts of Moab and Ammon ascended from the Dead Sea to the wilderness of Tekoa (2 Chron. 20: 16–20). Approaching by the same route the invading army from the East, at an earlier date, came to Engedi, where they smote the Amorites (Gen. 14: 7). From thence to the northern end of the Dead Sea the only practicable route would be by the ascent of Ziz. "This pass and cliff," says Professor Palmer, "have been from the days of Chedorlaomer and Abraham, the one ascent by which invaders from the south and east entered the hill country of Judea. As far as Engedi they could march by the shore without any obstacle; north of it the shore line is impracticable, even for footmen, and there are no paths by which beasts could be led up. Had they taken any of the openings south of Engedi this must have entailed a long march across a rough and almost waterless desert."

This region of towering cliffs, yawning caverns and awful gorges was known in Old Testament times as the "Wilderness of Engedi." Among these "rocks of the wild goats" King Saul hunted for David and his men: and it was in one of the caves of this mountain stronghold that David cut off the skirt of Saul's robe, while he lay helpless before him in unconscious slumber.

The fountain of Engedi ("Ain Jidy") bursts out from the foot of a huge boulder on a shelving terrace, 1,340 feet below the cliffs which overhang it and 500 feet above the surface of the Dead Sea. The temperature of the clear, full stream which flows from this source is 83° Fahr.; and its course, as it dashes in cascades over projecting rocks, or flows swiftly down the lower slopes of alluvium at the foot of the mountain, is strikingly indicated—in contrast with the barrenness and desolation around it—by a luxuriant growth of rich, tropical vegetation. "This oasis," says Dr. G. A. Smith, "bursts upon the traveller from one of the driest and most poisoned regions of our planet. Either he has ridden across Jeshimon, seven hours without a water spring, three with hardly a bush, when suddenly, over the edge of a precipice, 400 feet below him, he sees a river of verdure burst from the rock, and scatter itself, reeds, bush, trees and grass, down other 300 feet to a broad mile of gardens by the beach of the blue sea; or he has come along the coast, through evil sulphur smells, with the bitter sea on one side, the cliffs of the desert on the other, and a fiery sun overhead, when round a corner of the cliffs he sees the same broad fan of verdure open and slope before him. He passes up it, through gardens of cucumber and melon, small fields of wheat, and a scattered orchard, to a brake of reeds and high bushes with a few great trees. He hears what, perhaps, he has not heard for days—the rush of water; and then through the bush he sees the foam of a little waterspout, six feet high and almost two broad, which is only one branch of a pure, fresh stream that breaks from some boulders above on a shelf at the foot of the precipices. The verdure and water, so strange and sudden, with the exhilaration of the great view across the sea, produce the most generous impressions of this oasis, and tempt to the exaggeration of its fertility."

While we agree with the writer of this singularly realistic description as to the tendency to exaggeration amid such surroundings, it is evident from the variety and unique character of the vegetation which grows up amid its thickets and brakes, without direction or care, that it has possibilities under careful cultivation of becoming once more a far-renowned garden of choice fruits and fragrant spices,—the place of the palm-tree, the camphire, and the vine—as it was in the days of Solomon, and probably for many centuries before.

Its identification with Hazezon-tamar (Gen. 14: 7)—a designation older than the time of Abraham—is clearly indicated in 2 Chron. 20: 2; where it is referred to as "Hazezon-tamar, which is Engedi."

Just below the point where the fountain issues from the rock there are remains of broken walls, aqueducts and substantial buildings, but the ancient city of Engedi was on the small delta at the foot of the wady which conducts the water to the plain. Between these points there was, in former times, an orderly succession of ledges and terraces which caught the first rays of the rising sun, and were kept green and bright by the warm waters of the ever-flowing stream. Engedi was then, as it is now, a sheltered spot of unusual possibilities, with a climate of perpetual summer.

Among the thickets of shrubs, canes and vines which now cover this neglected spot, Canon Tristram found many gnarled acacias, the seyal or shittimwood of the desert; the "osher," or apple of Sodom (Calotropis procera); the hyssop, clinging to the moist walls of the cliff; the colocynth, or wild gourd of 2 Kings 4: 40; the retam, or broom, identical with the shrub (rothem) under which Elijah rested in the wilderness south of Beer-sheba; the salvadora persica, a tree with pungent seeds, belonging exclusively to tropical climes; and here and there a few clusters of the fragrant camphire—identical with the "henna" of oriental commerce—which was one of the choice products of this desert oasis nearly 3,000 years ago.

While there is no other region in Syria where such a wide expanse of rugged surface and dreary waste can be found, the Judean wilderness is not an utter desolation "without tree or shrub or sign of vegetation," as some writers, who have seen it only under the withering blight of the summer's sun, have described it. Throughout its extent, as already intimated, there are many places barren and wild, beyond description, where it is literally true that no waters murmur, no chirp of song-bird is heard, and no leaf nor blade of grass stirs in the breeze, but this is not true of the district as a whole.

In the Scriptures there are frequent references to the "*pastures of the wilderness.*" Like all the rest of Judea, this district is a pasture range for sheep and goats, but it is only available for this purpose, save in a few exceptional locations in the winter and early portion of the spring-time. At this season the slopes are thinly covered with grass, and spangled with flowers, and even amid the rugged "rocks of the wild goats," which border the Dead Sea, there are succulent herbs and clumps of thorny shrubs and little basins of green pasturage. The writer has seen a large flock of sheep and goats, under a shepherd's care, among the wild rocks which border the Wady en Nar between Mar Saba and the Dead Sea, and it is a well-known fact that the Bedawin tribes which claim this district as their peculiar heritage, find sustenance for their flocks, at certain seasons of the year, over the entire range of the wilderness section.

On the edge of the dreary waste east of Bethlehem, and sometimes far down on the desert slopes below, the youthful David kept his father's flock, defending them from the attacks of wild beasts, leading them into safe paths, and choosing out for them the best of the pasturage and the safest of the places among the strongholds of the rocks, for shelter and rest. Here the sheep are absolutely dependent upon the shepherd's care, and it is not without significance that our Lord chose this locality for the setting of the Parable of "The Lost Sheep." It was at the folding place "*in the wilderness*" that the shepherd missed the straying one and there he left the ninety and nine to go after that which was lost, until he found it. Nor is it without significance that we find the imagery of this rugged region in the "Shepherd Psalm" written by David the King in commemoration of Jehovah's goodness and never failing providential care. Amid the scenes with which he was familiar as a youth we get our best and truest conception of the Shepherd of Israel. Here,—as Dr. George Adams Smith has happily expressed it—" when you meet the guardian of the flock, sleepless, far-sighted, weather-beaten, armed, leaning on his staff, and looking out over his scattered sheep, every one of them on his heart, you understand why the shepherd of Judea sprang to the front in his people's history; why they gave his name to their king, and made him the symbol of Providence; why Christ took him as the type of self-sacrifice." It should be noted in this connection that the contrast between the appearance of the wilderness in the dry months of summer and the period already described is more marked than in any other portion of the land. With the passing of the "latter rains" the verdure of the hills begins to fade away into the brown tints of the desert, and, except in a few sheltered locations, the grasses, the leaves and the flowers are quickly shrivelled and scorched by the intense heat of the unclouded sun. From this time until the beginning of the time of the "former rains" the tawny hues of the desert are the prevailing colors, and the soil, which a little while before nourished the grasses and flowers, seems to have turned into dust and ashes.

The associations of the Wilderness of Judea are interwoven with the history of the Israelites from the beginning to the end of their national existence. They entered its northern limits under the leadership of Joshua to begin the conquest of the land; and in the wildest and most desolate portion of its southern border a little remnant of the survivors of the awful destruction at Jerusalem, made their last unavailing stand against the irresistible might of the legions of Rome.

The solemn grandeur and awe-inspiring scenes of this rugged region had their influence also in moulding the life and literature of the Hebrew people. Its borders were close to the chief cities of Judah and Benjamin and its unique features were familiar to unnumbered multitudes, who approached the Holy City from the north, during the great festival seasons, by way of the Jordan valley.

This was "the land not inhabited," yet always in view from the terraces of the Temple Hill, into which the scapegoat was led by the hand of a fit man, after the iniquities of the people had been confessed and symbolically laid upon his head.

It has been said with truth that "this howling waste came within reach of nearly every Jewish child, and was always in the face of the Hebrew prophets." The statement will apply with equal pertinency to the sacred poets, of whom David, the sweet singer of Israel is a conspicuous example. Here John the Baptist sought seclusion while preparing for his mission as the Forerunner of Messiah. As he mused amid these awful solitudes the fire burned, and thence he went forth in the spirit and power of Elijah to break the long silence which had followed the warning of Malachi and to summon the whole nation to repentance as a preparation for the coming of the Holy One.

To the same predestined place our Lord was led up by the Spirit after His baptism by John in the river of Jordan. "And He was there in the Wilderness,"—says the Evangelist Mark,—"forty days, tempted of Satan; and was with the wild beasts; and the angels ministered unto Him." This event, so wonderful in itself and so amazing in its significance and results, has made this old-time refuge of outlaws and wild beasts to be a hallowed place for all time.

V

SHECHEM AND ITS ENVIRONS

THE most conspicuous elevations along the line of the Patriarchal Highway from Judea to Galilee are the twin mountains, Ebal and Gerizim. The rugged summits of these celebrated mountains rise side by side on the western edge of the broad upland plain of Mukhna, in the very heart of the rich heritage of the children of Joseph.

As seen from the south or east they appear to be conical peaks, but in reality they are parallel ridges, running nearly east and west and terminating abruptly in rounded masses on the border of the plain. The distance between the bases of Ebal and Gerizim at this point is scarcely more than 500 yards. The long, narrow valley between the mountains has been known from time immemorial as the vale of Shechem. It enters the plain of Mukhna almost at right angles to its general direction and about one-third of the length from its northern end.

Nablus, the modern representative of the ancient city of Shechem, nestles amid a dark mass of luxuriant vegetation between the mountain ridges in the upper portion of the valley of Shechem. It is out of sight of the plain and nearly two miles distant from it. Shechem is almost

SHECHEM AND ITS ENVIRONS.

midway between Dan and Beersheba, and may be regarded as the central city of the middle section of Palestine. It is thirty miles from Jerusalem; thirty miles from Cesarea; thirty-three miles from Bethshan; eighteen from Jenin, and about sixteen from the nearest ford of the Jordan. The city overspreads a narrow watershed, which parts the rivulets, flowing from the bases of the mountains on either hand to east and west. At one point the streams, which flow from gushing fountains within the walls, run from the east gate to the Jordan. At another point a little farther to the west, they may be seen gliding swiftly in the opposite direction towards the plain of Sharon and the Mediterranean Sea. The inhabitants of Nablus boast of eighty springs of water within and around the city. It is probable that this number may be reduced by at least one-half, but there are few places to which the description, "well watered everywhere, even as the garden of the Lord," would more aptly apply. There is certainly no spot in Central Palestine which rivals this narrow valley in rich verdure, luxuriant vegetation, and luscious fruitage. It calls forth the admiration of travellers from every clime, and may be regarded as a typical representation of the natural beauty and extraordinary productiveness of "the good land" in its best estate. "There is a singularity about the vale of Shechem," says Van de Velde, "and that is the peculiar coloring which objects assume in it.

You know that wherever there is water the air becomes charged with watery particles, and that distant objects beheld through that medium seem to be enveloped in a pale blue or gray mist. It is precisely those atmospheric tints that we miss so much in Palestine. But in the vale of Shechem it is otherwise, at least in the morning and evening. Here the exhalations remain hovering among the branches and leaves of the olive-trees, and hence that lovely bluish haze. The valley is far from broad, not exceeding in some places a few hundred feet. This you find generally enclosed on all sides; here likewise the vapors are condensed. And so you advance under the shade of the foliage, along the living waters, and charmed by the melody of a host of singing birds—for they, too, know where to find the best quarters—while the perspective fades away, and is lost in the damp, vapory atmosphere."

Shechem has the singular honor of being *the oldest of all the sacred places* in the Promised Land. To this "place of Sichem" Abram came, with his flocks and herds, about forty centuries ago. It is probable that he crossed the Damieh ford of the Jordan near the mouth of the Jabbok, and thence followed the course of the Wady Farah to his camping ground by the oak of Moreh, in front of the city. Here he built an altar unto Jehovah, "who appeared unto him." Hitherto he had been seeking a land which the Lord had promised to show unto him, but now as he stood by this altar the promise was definitely made: "Unto thy seed will I give this land." Some two hundred years later his grandson, Jacob, came from Padan Aram, apparently over the same route from the highlands of Gilead, and pitched his tents on the broad plain in front of Shechem. With a view to a longer sojourn than that of Abram, and doubtless for the purpose of dwelling apart from the people of the land, Jacob purchased a portion of the ground which commands the entrance to the vale of Shechem, and here he pitched his tents and erected his altar.

During this sojourn the patriarch dug the well, which still bears his name, and which has marked this site through all succeeding generations. The place of the oak (or terebinth) which sheltered Abram has been identified with Belata, a little village a short distance due west of Jacob's Well. Under this oak, which was by Shechem, Jacob hid the strange gods, which some of the members of his household had brought with them from the other side of the Euphrates, before he renewed his covenant with Jehovah at Bethel. In this field Joseph wandered in search of his brethren, who had meanwhile removed to Dothan; and here, centuries after this event, he was buried in the presence of the assembled thousands of Israel.

After the conquest by Divine direction this "parcel of ground" became the inheritance of the children of Joseph. The traditional site of the burial-place of Joseph is on a slight elevation about four hundred yards north of Jacob's Well.

It is almost in the middle of the mouth of the valley of Shechem. The location accords with the Biblical narrative, and for many centuries it has been held in reverence by Jews, Samaritans, Moslems and Christians. At the base of Mount Ebal, a little farther to the north, is the modern village of Askar, which has been satisfactorily identified with Sychar. It occupies the site of an older town. Sychar is described in John's gospel as "a city of Samaria near to the parcel of ground that Jacob gave to his son, Joseph."

The place of the grand national assembly, where all the tribes of Israel were gathered after the conquest, to hear and ratify the "book of the Law of God which Moses had written," was in the valley of Shechem between its mouth, at Jacob's Well, and the eastern limit of the ancient city. Next to the giving of the law at Sinai, this was the most sublime spectacle and impressive service in the history of the covenant people. It is a noteworthy fact that two breaks, or lateral valleys, directly opposite each other, have formed natural amphitheatres on either slope of the mountains, which seem to have been prepared for such an occasion. The narrative distinctly affirms that the people "stood on this side and that of the ark; half of them in front of Mount Gerizim, and half of them over against Mount Ebal; as Moses the servant of the Lord had commanded." There is no intimation that either the readers or those who responded were on the top of the mountain.

The objection sometimes urged on this supposition has no support in the story of this impressive service, nor in the topography of the site where it took place. Says Dr. Thomson:—
"That was the most august assembly of the kind the sun ever shone upon; and I never stand in that narrow plain, with Ebal and Gerizim rising on either hand to the sky, without involuntarily recalling the scene. I have shouted to hear the responsive echo, and fancied how impressive it must have been when the loud-voiced Levites proclaimed from the cliffs of Ebal, 'Cursed be the man that maketh any graven or molten image, an abomination unto the Lord.' And then the tremendous Amen! tenfold louder from the mighty congregation, rising and swelling, and reechoing from Ebal to Gerizim and from Gerizim to Ebal."

In this valley at a later period, Joshua gathered all the tribes of Israel to listen to his farewell charge, and here in the most solemn manner the people renewed their covenant with Jehovah, engaging to serve Him only, and to put away the strange gods which were among them. "And Joshua wrote these words in the book of the law of God, and took a great stone, and set it up there under an oak, that was by the sanctuary of the Lord." This stone or pillar of witness was the place where the men of Shechem afterwards proclaimed the usurper Abimelech, as king. There can scarcely be a doubt that the oak referred to in these passages was the famous tree which had sheltered Abraham and Jacob centuries before. On Mount Gerizim, Jotham, the only surviving son of the warrior-judge, Gideon, uttered in the hearing of the people of Shechem, the fable of the talking trees. This quaint homily, the first of its kind recorded in history, embodied a scathing rebuke to the men of Shechem for their ingratitude and folly in choosing the murderer of his brethren to be their king; and a presage of the calamity as well, which was certain to overtake them in the end. "It is pleasant," says Dr. Thomson, "to see around us from this standpoint, and blending with the diversified foliage of the valley beyond, the olive, the fig, the vine, and the bramble, apparently as capable to-day to assume their part in a parable, or give point to a rebuke, as they were in the time of Jotham."

At Shechem, after the death of Solomon, there was another great assembly of Israel which resulted in the rejection of Rehoboam, and the crowning of Jeroboam, another usurper, by the representatives of the ten tribes. Following this act Shechem became for a time the capital of the northern kingdom. Long afterwards, when the ten tribes had been carried away into captivity by the Assyrians, Shechem became the chief seat, and sacred city, of the Samaritans. With a view to rival and if possible supplant the worship of the Jews at Jerusalem, the sect of the Samaritans, reinforced by some noted Jews, who had been expelled from Jerusalem for unlawful marriages, built a great national temple on Mount Gerizim. This temple, erected B. C. 300, was destroyed by the Jews about 130 years before the birth of Christ. Its ruins crowned the height of Gerizim when Jesus passed this way into Galilee, and to this spot the woman of Samaria pointed when she said:—"Our fathers worshipped in this mountain; and ye say that Jerusalem is the place where men ought to worship." Notwithstanding the destruction of their temple, the Samaritans continued to worship on the summit of Gerizim; and it is a notable fact that they have observed the Passover on this mountain, in strict accord with the Jewish ritual, in almost continuous succession, year by year, from the destruction of Jerusalem until this day. This is the only place on the face of the earth where this sacred festival has been celebrated continuously during this time after the manner of the Jewish ritual. The Samaritan sect now numbers only 160 persons all told, but they still have a synagogue in Shechem—the repository of the sacred roll of the Pentateuch, undoubtedly of great age:—and the pathway up to the summit of the mountain deeply worn by the tread of their forefathers of many generations has never been effaced nor obscured. With them as with us the spot of greatest interest in this cluster of sacred places is the site of Jacob's Well. They have never lost sight of it, and in a sense have been its guardians since the beginning of the Christian era. The unbroken traditions of the Jews, Moslems and Christians accord with this testimony.

Since the fourth century its site has been marked, and also protected from the sand and soil which has gathered around it, by a small church or chapel. The present structure is probably a reconstruction of the fourth century chapel, or it may be the crypt of this ancient church. In any case it covers the same ground and bears silent testimony to the reliability of this identification. In view of all the evidence at hand, it may be confidently asserted that no spot of ground within the limits of the Holy Land has been more certainly identified than the site of this wayside well at the entrance of the vale of Shechem. A few years ago the only visible opening to the well was a hole, partly covered by a great stone, in the floor of the crypt or subterranean chapel. To reach this opening it was necessary to clamber down into this chamber some eight or ten feet, through a rift in its vaulted roof.

To Dr. C. A. Barclay, long a resident missionary in Jerusalem, the credit is due for the discovery of the real mouth of Jacob's Well. While visiting this place in 1881, in company with his wife, he noticed a dark crack in the stone floor a few feet from the opening already described. Upon removing some of the stones and a mass of accumulated rubbish, he was able to trace part of a curved aperture in a great stone beneath him. Deeply interested in this discovery, he called some workmen to his aid and, after removing an immense mass of blockage, the original mouth of the well was cleared. "It is impossible," says

Dr. Barclay, "to describe our feelings as we gazed down the open well, and sat on that ledge on which doubtless the Saviour rested, and felt with our fingers the grooves in the stone caused by the ropes by which the water pots were drawn up."

The associations of this place carry us far back in the world's history amid pastoral scenes and patriarchal customs, but the event which the Apostle John so graphically describes, transcends all others in interest and importance. Here in the very beginning of His public ministry Jesus revealed Himself to a perplexed inquirer as the long promised Messiah, the Saviour of the *world*. By this hallowed spot to-day we may see all the distinctive features of the landscape on which His eyes rested nineteen centuries ago. Here are the twin mountains, which rise as of old abruptly from the great plain; the narrow vale of Shechem which lies between; the wide expanse of the vast grain field which stretches far away to north and south; the sites of Salim, Sychar and Shechem within easy reach; the place of worship on the summit of the sacred mountain of the Samaritans; the dusty road on which the Redeemer travelled, skirting the base of this mountain; and, stranger than all, the stone curb—hidden from view for well-nigh fifteen centuries, and now brought to the light of day—on which for a few moments Jesus rested His weary limbs at the midday hour. There came to the well at this hour a woman of Samaria. In the incidents which follow we may see how the Good Shepherd sought and found, on that memorable day, a lost sheep among the mountains of Samaria.

VI

THE PLAIN OF GENNESARET

BETWEEN Magdala—now known as Mejdel—and Khan Minyeh the Mountains of Galilee recede from the Lake, in an almost semicircular sweep, leaving a beautiful, crescent-shaped plain. Its extent along the coast is three and a quarter miles; its breadth at the widest part is one and one-eight miles. The cliffs which border the plain on the south extend almost to the margin of the lake. On the north it is wholly cut off from the lowland strip beyond by a spur or promontory, which runs down to the water. The Arabs call this mountain-girdled tract El Ghuweir, the "Little Ghor." Its identity with the "Land of Gennesareth" (Matt. 14: 34; Mark 6: 53) is unquestioned. The limits correspond closely with the measurements given by Josephus and in the wild tangle of tropical undergrowth, grasses and vines, which now covers its desolation one may readily see the proofs of the extraordinary fertility, which once made it the garden spot of Northern Palestine.

The shore-line of the Gennesaret plain is slightly embayed and the beach, which slopes gradually to the water's edge, is thickly strewn with myriads of tiny, pearly-white shells. At some points this silvery strand is "a texture of shells and pebbles so minute as to resemble sand"; at others cart loads of delicately-formed semi-transparent shells could be gathered up. On the landward side of this beautiful pathway by the sea, an almost continuous hedge of oleanders and tropical thorns holds back a confused mass of wild, luxuriant vegetation. There are no fences and no groups of trees to obstruct the vision between the limits of the sea and the mountains; and at several points of view the whole plain and its borderings may be seen at a glance. Three deeply-cleft wadies or ravines break through the encircling barrier of hills on the western side. These are known as The Wadies Hamam, Rubudiyeh and Amud. From each of these the drainage of the adjacent highlands is carried, in perennial streams, across the plain to the lake. The traveller going northward crosses these brooks from the mountains at almost regular intervals of space between Magdala and Khan Minyeh. Their course from the mouths of the ravines whence they issue, may be readily traced by a rank growth of willows, oleanders and marsh mallows, which line the banks and ofttimes conceal the streams that glide beneath them.

The Wady Amud opens upon this lowland region near Khan Minyeh. It is a long narrow gorge noted for its wild and savage grandeur. The stream which it carries to the plain takes its rise near Jebel Jermuk, the highest peak of the mountains of Naphtali. In some places the cliffs

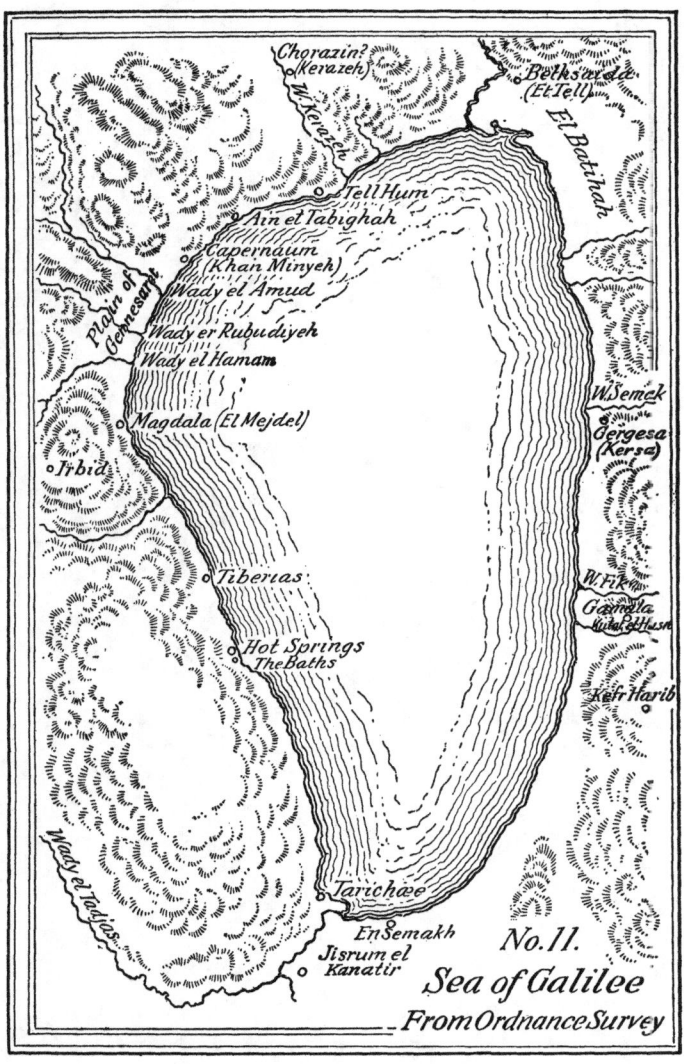

SEA OF GALILEE.

rise precipitously from the edge of the stream to the height of nearly 1,000 feet. The upper portion of this ravine is called Wady Leimon.

The brook which flows from the Wady er Rubudiyeh through the centre of the plain is the largest of the mountain streams and its waters are carried by means of artificial canals to the north and south for purposes of irrigation.

The Wady el Hamam opens upon the plain a short distance westward of the site of Magdala. The rugged cliffs which border it on either side rise perpendicularly to the height of more than 1,000 feet. A labyrinth of caves, with connecting passages cut into the face of the rock on the south side of the ravine, has been for many centuries an impregnable stronghold of defense to the oppressed, as well as a favorite hiding-place for outlaws and robber bands. The higher tier of caves can only be reached from above by means of ropes. In the time of Herod the Great a large body of outlaws, who had hitherto defied the authority of Rome, were besieged in this stronghold. After a series of desperate struggles they were at length destroyed or driven out by companies of soldiers let down from the dizzy heights above in great chests strongly bound with hoops of iron.

These storied caves became, at a later period, the favorite abodes of anchorites and hermits. At the present time myriads of wild pigeons have their nesting places in the holes and caves of these walls of rock. Hence the name: Wady el Hamam, the Valley of Pigeons or Doves. Hattin, the traditional mount of the Beatitudes, is a conspicuous landmark at the upper end of the valley, and its twin peaks or horns, may be distinctly seen through the open mouth of the gorge from several view-points on the lake and plain. The great caravan route from Esdraelon and the South to Damascus follows the line of the old Roman road through Wady Hamam to Khan Minyeh and thence northward over the hills of Naphtali. This was the direct road from Cana to Capernaum in the Saviour's day, and He must have often journeyed over it during the period of the Galilean ministry.

Between the Hamam and Rubudiyeh valleys a copious fountain known as Ain Mudawarah bursts forth from the foot of the hills and sends a stream of clear, refreshing water across the plain to the lake. A circular basin or reservoir of stone ninety-six feet in diameter encloses the spring. "The water," says Dr. Robinson, "is perhaps two feet deep, beautifully limpid and sweet, bubbling up and flowing out rapidly in a large stream to water the plain below. Numerous small fish were sporting in the basin, which is so thickly surrounded by trees and brushwood that a stranger would be apt to pass by without noticing it." Another notable fountain (Ain et Tin) rises at the southern base of the Khan Minyeh cliff and runs eastward into the lake. It is too near the level of the lake to be utilized for the irrigation of any considerable portion of the plain, but its brief course seaward is marked by luxuriant pasture beds of grass and clover. Dr. Robinson makes special mention of this tract of clover around the fountain and along the shore, and adds that it had a freshness and verdure such as he saw nowhere else in Palestine. "It was a luxury to rest in it." "These pastures of Minyeh," says Burckhardt, "are proverbial for their richness." Near the shore the stream from Ain et Tin widens out into a marsh "skirted with oleanders and choked with wavy tufts of the beautiful, tall papyrus of Egypt."

It has been shown conclusively, as the result of careful explorations, that the abundant water supply, which now runs to waste from the great fountain of Tabighah, three-quarters of a mile north of Khan Minyeh, was formerly conveyed by an aqueduct into the Gennesaret plain. An octagonal reservoir of great strength surrounds this spring-head, which is notable as the largest of its kind in Galilee. The water was formerly raised within this basin, by means of mechanical contrivances, about twenty feet to the level of the aqueduct. "After leaving the reservoir," says Colonel Wilson, "the aqueduct can be traced at intervals, following the contour of the ground to the point where it crossed the bed of two water-courses on arches, of which the piers may still be seen; it then turns down towards the lake, and runs along the hillside on the top of a massive retaining wall, of which fifty or sixty yards remain, and lastly passes round the Khan

Minyeh cliff by a remarkable excavation in the solid rock, which has been noticed by all travellers. The elevation of the aqueduct at this point is sufficient to have enabled the water brought by it to irrigate the whole plain, and although we could only trace it for a few yards inland, it was not improbably carried right round the head of the plain: the same causes which have almost obliterated it in the small plain of Tabighah would fully account for its disappearance in Gennesareth."

In the light of this direct evidence, confirmed by the researches of Kitchener (now Major General Kitchener) and Dr. Selah Merrill, it is in the highest degree probable that this is the famous fountain of Capernaum, mentioned by Josephus, which poured its life-giving streams over the beautiful and fertile "land of Gennesar." If this be so, it follows that the gardens and fields which it enriched and beautified, first of all, were in the belt that immediately surrounded Capernaum, the lakeside home of Jesus. In the period of the Romans, Gennesaret was the focus of life and activity of one of the most thickly settled provinces of Palestine. Its towns and villages were thickly clustered on plain and hillside and every foot of the land was skillfully cultivated. With a climate mild as Egypt—fitly described as "a harmonious blending of the seasons"—with a loamy soil of unusual depth and richness, and with an abundant water supply, which was extended over every portion of its surface, it is no marvel that it was known far and wide as the garden spot of Palestine. "Along the lake of Gennesar"—says the Jewish historian—"extends the district of like name, wondrous in natural beauty. Such is the fertility of the soil that it rejects no plant, and so genial is the climate that it suits every variety; the walnut, which delights in a wintry climate, grows here luxuriantly, together with the palm-tree which is nourished by heat, and near to those are figs and olives to which a milder atmosphere has been assigned. One might style this an ambitious effort of nature, doing violence to herself in bringing together plants of discordant habits, and an amiable rivalry of the seasons, each as it were asserting its right to the soil; for it not only possesses the extraordinary virtue of nourishing fruits of opposite climes, but also contains a continual supply of them. Thus it produces those most royal of all, the grape and the fig, during ten months, without intermission, while the other varieties ripen the year round; for besides being favored by the genial temperature of the air, it is irrigated by a highly fertilizing spring, called Capharnaum by the people of the country" (Bell. Jud. III, 10, 8).

The contrast between this glowing description and the present condition of the Gennesaret plain is painfully apparent. Between the irregular mounds on its northern border, which cover almost all that remains of the once prosperous and highly favored city of Capernaum, and the cluster of thirty odd mud hovels, which represents the town of Mary Magdalene on its southern edge, there is not a single permanent human habitation. Except an occasional patch of a few rods square cleared of its dense undergrowth for a season's crop, by the fellaheen or a migratory band of Bedouins, the entire plain has reverted to its primitive condition. The hand of the diligent husbandman no longer directs the growth of its meads and slopes and the fruitful garden has become a wilderness. Its almost impenetrable thickets of undergrowth, in which delicate grasses and myriads of richly-tinted flowers struggle with brambles and thorns are suggestive only of an Eden-run-wild. Long ago have the walnut and the fig, the pomegranate and the vine been crowded out by hardy plants of meaner growth; and the solitary palm which marks the ruined site of Magdala appears to be the only survivor of all the orchards and groves which were once its pride and glory.

Amid all these changes and desolations the framework and distinguishing characteristics of this natural amphitheatre yet remain. There is no other place on earth where so much of the divinely-beautiful life of Jesus was seen; where so many of His mighty works were done. Here we may read page after page of "the Fifth Gospel," torn indeed and soiled, but still legible; and there is not an incident or an expression in the story of the evangelists that does not harmonize with these open pages, as they lie in

SITE OF MAGDALA—THE HOME OF MARY MAGDALENE.
The curve of the bay can best be seen from this point.

the clear sunlight between the mountains and the sea.

Most beautifully has the Master woven the several details and peculiarities of this varied landscape into the texture of the series of Parables, which belong to the period of His early ministry. In these pictorial representations of the Kingdom of Grace we have the imagery, the landscape-coloring, and many of the special features of the Gennesaret of to-day. A case in point is the familiar parable of the sower. Here, as of old, the sower goes forth from village or hamlet near by, to sow. As he scatters the seed over his little patch of prepared ground, the birds of the air, which have their nesting places in the holes and caves of the cliffs above, circle about his head and watch eagerly for the opportunity to catch away the uncovered grains, which fall upon the well-trodden pathway that leads through or alongside his field. In the midst of the "good ground," which if carefully tilled would still bring forth sixty, and, in choice locations, one hundredfold, there is a ledge of rock covered from sight by the rich soil, but it fails after a time to nourish the plants which grow upon it, because it has "no deepness of earth." At another point there is a little clump of encroaching briars and thorns which choke the springing grain and render it unfruitful.

"The image of corn-fields generally," says Dean Stanley, "must have been always present to the eye of the multitudes on shore, as well as of the Master and disciples in the boat. 'The earth bringing forth fruit of itself'—'the blade, the ear, the full corn in the ear'—'the reapers coming with their sickles for the harvest,' could never be out of place in the Plain of Gennesaret." Other illustrations of like character, drawn from familiar objects about Him on plain or lake or mountainside, have their counterparts within this limited area. Here in very surety "one great memory lingers," and every spot is hallowed ground. Here where the desert places to which He went betimes for communion and prayer, trench so closely upon the fertile fields; where the sunbeams play upon the surface of the clear blue waters as they ripple along the pearly beach; where every natural feature is pleasing to the eye and only the labor and skill of men are needed to make it again the garden of the Lord, was the favored place, we may well believe, "where Jesus loved so much to be"; and where He spent the busiest, happiest hours of His earthly life. We can hardly be wrong in saying that it was to this place of hallowed memories also that Jesus came to meet His disciples after His resurrection.

> " O Saviour gone to God's right hand,
>   But the same Saviour still;
> Graved on Thy heart is this lovely strand,
>   And every fragrant hill."

VII

THE SEA OF GALILEE

The usual approach to the Sea of Galilee is by the old roadway, deeply worn by the tread of many generations, which leads down from Nazareth, by way of Cana, to Tiberias. From a notable outlook on one of the lower levels in this descent, the traveller gets his first view of the lake and its environs. As seen under a cloudless sky, and in the fresh spring-time, from this standpoint—nearly a thousand feet above the water—the picture is singularly beautiful, as well as deeply impressive. The sweep of vision is limited to the northern half of the Sea, but it includes almost all of the localities, which have been hallowed by the presence and ministry of Jesus.

From the heights of Safed, three thousand feet above the water level, the whole of the mountain-rimmed basin of Galilee may be seen at a glance.

In the Old Testament it is known as the Sea of Chinnereth or Chinneroth; in the Gospels it is called the Lake of Gennesaret, the Sea of Galilee, and the Sea of Tiberias. In John's gospel only do we find the latter name; and this fact has its most natural explanation on the assumption that this apostle wrote after the city of Tiberias had risen to importance, as the capital of Galilee.

The most noteworthy feature of this inland sea is its deep depression. It lies 682 feet below the level of the Mediterranean, and the mountains which gracefully curve around it, shutting it in at every point, except where the Jordan makes its entrance and exit, vary in height from 1,300 to 2,000 feet. On the eastern side the mountains rise abruptly from the plain which borders the lake, to the level of the Bashan plateau; and the general impression is that of a bare rugged wall of rock, cleft here and there by deeply-gashed torrent beds. In these are occasional patches of green, but the prevailing colors are the red and brown of the vast masses of bare basaltic rock.

On the western side the range is broken into rounded hills and grass-covered slopes, which in some places, terminate abruptly as they approach the margin of the sea. Between the base of the enclosing hills and the coast line there is an almost continuous belt of green lowland, varying in width from a ribbon-like strip to a generous expanse of one or two miles. "The shore line, for the most part regular, is broken in the north into a series of little bays of exquisite beauty; nowhere more beautiful than at Gennesareth, where the beaches, nearly white with myriads of minute shells, are on one side washed by the limpid waters of the lake, and on the other shut in by a fringe of oleanders, "rich in May with

NORTHERN BASIN OF GENNESARET FROM HIGHLANDS OF GALILEE.

The Horns of Hattin appear in the foreground of the picture.

their blossoms red and bright" (Our Work in Palestine, p. 184).

Over the rim of the mountain wall northward the prospect is closed by the towering heights of Hermon. From every outlook south of Magdala the cloudy coronal, and snowy mantle of this majestic mountain may be seen; and at some points it seems so near that it can hardly be distinguished from the contour of the mountain mass which overshadows the margin of the lake.

In outline the Sea of Galilee is an irregular oval, the larger end being at the north. Its extreme length is twelve and a quarter miles. Its greatest width—from Magdala to Khersa (Gergesa)—is six and three-quarter miles. The maximum depth, as ascertained by recent measurements, is one hundred and fifty-six feet. The water is bright and clear, and is almost as delicate a blue as the Bay of Naples. In its ordinary condition it is a water-mirror of rare beauty and reflective power; and the play of the lights and shadows on its surface and surrounding hills, amid the ever-varying atmospheric changes, from sunrise to sunset, greatly enhances the charm of its natural features. In the rich warm glow of the setting sun, which seems to impart to this lake-region a peculiar glory, the beloved disciple must often have witnessed a counterpart of that scene in holy vision, which he describes as "a sea of glass mingled with fire."

While Galilee is usually "a calm reposing sea,"

it is, nevertheless, subject at times to violent tempests which sweep down through the ravines from the heights above, with scarcely a moment's notice. Says Dr. Thomson: "Small as the lake is, and placid in general, as a molten mirror, I have repeatedly seen it quiver, and leap and boil like a caldron, when driven by fierce winds from the eastern mountains, and the waves ran high— high enough to fill or cover the ships, as Matthew has it." Sir Charles Wilson gives a very interesting account of a sudden storm, which he watched from the ruins of Gamala on the eastern side as it swept rapidly across a portion of the sea and lifted the placid waters into a bright sheet of foam. "The effect," he says, "of half the lake in perfect rest, while the other half was in wild confusion, was extremely grand; it would have fared badly with any light craft caught in mid-lake by the storm; and we could not help thinking of that memorable occasion on which the storm is so graphically described as 'coming down' on the lake."

While the Sea of Galilee abounds, as of old, in choice varieties of fish, the fishing industry, once so important, is well-nigh extinct. The best fishing grounds are still at the northern end, near Capernaum and Tabighah, where the fish sometimes appear in shoals in countless numbers. "The lake absolutely swarms with fish," says Canon Tristram, "and the shoals may often be seen in dark masses, which as their top fins appear on the surface, look at a distance as though a violent shower were rippling the surface for an extent of an acre or more." At the present time there are possibly less than half a dozen rude fishing boats on the lake, but in the time of Christ it was covered with vessels large and small of every description. Ship building was one of the important industries at Tarichæa, a large city south of Tiberias; and here, on one occasion, Josephus collected 230 ships, which he manned with sailors, to attack Tiberias from the lakeside.

In a valuable article on the shipping of the Sea of Galilee, Dr. Merrill says: "Josephus' words, in describing different vessels on the Sea of Galilee, are: *Naus*, ship; *ploion*, vessel; *skapha*, a boat smaller than a vessel; *schedia*, a light boat, sometimes a raft; *alias*, fishing boat. *Naus* is used but once in the New Testament, and that in connection with Paul's shipwreck. *Skapha* is used, but only of the boat which belonged to the ploion. *Ploion* is the word which the evangelists invariably use of the Sea of Galilee, except in a few instances where, to indicate a vessel of smaller size, they use its diminutive, *ploiarion*. In John 22:23, *ploiarion* is rendered "boat," but elsewhere, as in Mark 3:9, "little ship." The Authorized Version always renders *ploion* by "ship." In this they are more consistent than the Revisers have been, who in every case in the gospels (forty-seven times) render it by "boat," while in the Acts and elsewhere they render it by "ship." They can present no reason from grammar, etymology, or textual criticism, to justify them in rendering *ploion* by "ship" when the passage refers to Cesarea-on-the-Sea, and by "boat" when the passage refers to Tiberias or Capernaum. Such passages as Matthew 14:29, "Peter went down out of the *ploion*," and Mark 6:51, "Christ went up into the *ploion*, would seem to be sufficient evidence that something else was meant than what English-speaking people ordinarily mean by the term boat."

This argument, so convincingly presented, is in keeping with the fact that some of the vessels, at least, in which Jesus sailed over the lake were large enough to carry Himself and His disciples—the inference being that *all* of the apostolic band were with Him.

The Jordan descends from Lake Huleh to the Galilean basin, a distance of eleven miles, through a narrow gorge in a succession of rapids or cascades. For the greater part of this distance the descent is more than ninety feet to the mile. From the gateway of the hills the river emerges, a foaming, swirling torrent, crosses the belt of the coast plain, some two miles in breadth, and entering the sea passes through it, as does the Rhine through the Sea of Constance. For a considerable distance its course may be traced by its turbid waters, but at length it is lost to sight and hushed to rest in the bosom of the lake; and ere it passes out on its downward plunge to the Dead Sea, it is clear as the waves which ripple along the beach of the Gennesaret plain.

The topography and characteristic features of the coasts of Galilee can be studied to best advantage by making the circuit of the lake. The widest space between the surrounding hills and the water is at or near the inlet of the Jordan. The greater portion of this tract lies on the eastern side of the river, and is known as the Plain of Batihah, or Butaiha. It is somewhat larger than the Gennesaret plain, and is regarded as its counterpart in outline, general appearance and fertility. Near the lake there are numerous bogs and swampy patches, but the higher ground is a meadow-like tract, which yields a rich harvest wherever it is carefully cultivated. This was in the territory ruled by Philip the Tetrarch, and here he rebuilt and beautified the village of Bethsaida, raising it to the dignity of a city and naming it Julias, in honor of the daughter of the reigning Emperor. The probable scene of the miraculous feeding of the multitude was on the eastern edge of the plain, which seems to have been in the past, as it is at the present time, a desert or uninhabited region.

South of the plain of Batihah there is an unbroken border of level coast, seldom less than half a mile in width, which extends to the south end of the lake. The most notable contraction of the coast along this line is at Ghersa, the probable site of Gergesa, directly opposite Magdala on the western side. In the vicinity of this landing-place was the scene of the healing of the fierce demoniac and the destruction of the herd of swine. "The site," says Dr. Thomson, "is within a few rods of the shore, and a mountain rises directly above it, in which are ancient tombs; out of some of them the man possessed of the devils may have issued to meet Jesus. The lake is so near the base of the mountain at this place that a herd of swine feeding above it, seized with a sudden panic, would rush madly down the declivity, those behind tumbling over and thrusting forward those before, and, as there is no space to recover on the narrow plain between the base of the mountain and the lake, they would crowd headlong into the water and perish." To this description Dr. Thomson adds the statement that wild hogs abound at this place, and in a state as wild and fierce as though they were still "possessed."

The deepest furrow in the hills on this side is the Wady Fik, which enters the lake three miles below Ghersa. On the precipitous heights above are the ruins of Gamala (Kulat-el Husn), a well-nigh impregnable stronghold, famous for the desperate resistance its defenders made to the Romans.

The break in the hills through which the Jordan passes out of the Sea of Galilee is about four miles wide. It issues near the southwest corner and for a short distance runs nearly west. A ruined bridge of ten arches marks the crossing of the old Roman road from Tiberias to Gadara and the regions beyond. West of the Jordan on a little peninsula covered with ruins is the site of

TIBERIAS BY THE SEA OF GALILEE.

Tarichæa, now called Kerak. This is the only position on the coast, says Dr. Smith, which now suits Josephus's description of Tarichæa as washed on more than one side by the sea. From this point to the Hot Springs near Tiberias, a distance of four or five miles, the hills close down to the lake, leaving only a narrow margin of coastland. Tiberias nestles in a semicircular recess, which extends for a mile or more along the shore. Its ruins cover acres of ground, and recent researches have shown that the enclosing wall was nearly three miles in circumference. Between Tiberias and Magdala the hills again come down almost to the water's edge, except at one point where there is a slight expanse at the mouth of a ravine. On this level space some ruins of an ancient town have been found. The proposed identification of this site with Dalmanutha has met with some favor, inasmuch as it seems to have been near the border of Magdala, but there is no *positive* evidence in favor of this identification. The plain of Gennesaret, as already noted, extends from Magdala to Khan Minyeh. Beyond the spur of rock which forms its northern border lies Tabighah, the probable site of Bethsaida of Galilee. Tell Hum, which Robinson and others have identified with Chorazin, is a mile and a half farther along the coast. A journey of two and a half miles from this site brings us to the Jordan and completes the circuit.

In the time of our Lord not less than nine prosperous cities, with numerous outlying villages and villas, were scattered along this lowland belt. "As the Dead Sea is girdled by an almost countless hedge of driftwood," says Dr. Smith, "so the Sea of Galilee is girdled by a scarcely less continuous belt of ruins,—the drift of her ancient towns."

Dr. Selah Merrill, who spent weeks upon the shores of this silent sea, and had exceptional advantages for the study of its environs, gives the following testimony concerning the remarkable diversity of its natural features: "At every two or three miles of travel a new picture presents itself, so that, were an artist to go around the Sea of Galilee and make a collection of views, illustrating its shores, plains, streams, springs, hills, castles, and grander mountains which look down upon it from a distance, the result would be a wonderful surprise, certainly to those who are not familiar with this region, as showing the variety and beauty of scenes of nature that were constantly before the eyes of our Lord." Amid all the changes and desolations, which have well-nigh obliterated the works of man, the outlines and groundwork of its natural features still remain. Its fair expanse of waters, gleaming in the sunlight, like an opal set in emeralds; its pearly beach and charming bays; its rippling wavelets and crystal depths; its encircling plains and outer rim of rugged mountain walls combine to reproduce the very picture, in all its essential details, upon which the eyes of Jesus rested long centuries ago.

There may be other lakes more pleasing to the eye, with surroundings more picturesque or grand, but to the Christian Galilee, made blessedly familiar by the story of the evangelists, is next to the Holy City—the most hallowed spot on earth. Here by mountainside and lakeside the Glorious One who came to save preached the gospel of the kingdom; healed the sick, cleansed the lepers, opened the eyes of the blind; cast out demons, raised the dead, comforted the sorrowing, gave rest to the weary and heavy laden, calmed the raging winds and waves by a word, and made of the unstable waters a pathway for His feet, that He might come to the help of His imperilled disciples.

"What this lake region has lost in population and activity," says Dean Farrar, "it has gained in solemnity and interest. If every vestige of human habitation should disappear from beside it, and the jackal and the hyena should howl about the shattered fragments of the synagogues where Christ taught, yet the fact that He chose it as the scene of His opening ministry will give a sense of sacredness and pathos to its lonely waters till time shall be no more."

VIII

"HIS OWN CITY"

CAPERNAUM, by the Lake of Galilee, was the favorite dwelling-place of our Lord during the greater part of His public ministry. It was "His own city" by choice; and, as a result of that choice, it became the focus of His busy life by the lake, the birthplace of His church, the central pulpit of His teaching, and the central station of His missionary tours. Dr. Hanna makes mention of nine departures from and returns to Capernaum in the course of our Lord's Galilean ministries. Three of these were extensive tours through the towns and villages of the district; and five or six were more limited ones. As a recognized citizen of Capernaum Jesus paid tribute and frequently taught in the synagogue. When the people gathered around Him in crowds, insomuch that there was no room to receive them, He withdrew to the seaside close at hand, or taught them from a fishing vessel moored a little distance from the shore.

At Nazareth Jesus had enjoyed the privileges and shared the common experiences of household life with brothers and sisters, but from the time that He left this home of His childhood and youth He had not where to lay His head. In this city by the lake, to which Jesus brought such priceless blessings, He had no house that He could call His own. He had a richer possession here, however, in the wealth of love and affection bestowed upon Him by a few faithful followers and devoted friends, who gladly received Him into their houses and esteemed it a high honor and privilege to minister to His necessities. The house of Simon Peter seems to have been His home—in so far as He could have a home on earth—during this period of unselfish and almost incessant labors. Among the friends of Jesus, at this time resident in Capernaum, were Andrew and Peter; the mother-in-law of Peter, whom He had brought back from the gates of death by a touch of His hand; James and John, the sons of Zebedee; Matthew, the convert from the ranks of the Publicans; the nobleman of Herod's court, who, after the healing of his son, believed in Christ with his whole house; and many nameless disciples, also, who, like this nobleman's son, or the paralytic in Simon's house, had been healed in body and soul by the word or touch of Jesus.

Three of the evangelists have given us a record of the labors and beneficent ministries which filled one Sabbath day in Capernaum. As the evening time drew near the interest which had been awakened among the people increased and soon "all the city was gathered together" at the door of Simon's house: "and all they that had any sick with divers diseases brought them unto Him; and He laid His hands on every one of them and healed them " (Matt. 8: 14–17; Mark 1: 21–31; Luke 4: 33–41).

Capernaum in the time of Christ was a prosperous commercial city on one of the great highways from Egypt to Damascus. It was the centre of the local fisheries and an important shipping port on the lake. It had a customhouse, a notable synagogue, built by a friendly Roman centurion, and a castle or garrison manned by Roman soldiers. Here Jesus came into contact with men of every class, nationality and vocation, and thus prepared the way for the extension of His Kingdom, in later days, throughout the Roman world. The western shore of the Sea of Galilee, especially the Land of Gennesaret, was at this time a region of extraordinary beauty and fertility. There is abundant evidence that it was a densely populated district, thickly dotted over with prosperous cities and villages and all astir with life and activity. "In His day," says Dr. Selah Merrill, "the lake was full of fish and covered with boats. The wheat fields on the surrounding slopes yielded abundant harvests, and the plains produced the choicest fruits. Caravans and travellers crowded the highways, the shores were covered with people, and the entire basin presented a scene of life and activity such as was true of few other places in the world, and which it is difficult now for even the imagination to reproduce. It was in this beautiful region, and among its busy men, that our Lord chose His home, and did many of His wonderful works." "Nowhere," says another writer, "except in the capital itself, could He have found such a sphere for His works and words of mercy; from no other centre could 'His fame' have so gone throughout all Syria; nowhere else could He have so drawn around Him the vast multitudes who hung on His lips."

The contrast between this place in that day of prosperity and privilege and the utter desolation and abandonment of the present is an impressive commentary on the solemn and significant words in which Jesus, at length, pronounced its doom. It had privileges such as had not been enjoyed by any other city on earth, but its busy habitants neglected the day of their merciful visitation and rejected their heaven-sent King. Except a little company of devoted followers, the people of Capernaum were indifferent to the claims of the spiritual kingdom, which Jesus had come to establish in their midst, and the gracious words which they heard and the wonderful works which they witnessed, day by day, made no permanent impression on mind or heart. They saw and they heard but they repented not. "To any thoughtful student of the Gospel History," says Dean Stanley, "it would have seemed that, of all places there recorded, the scene of our Lord's permanent residence, of His home for the three most important years of His life, would have been regarded as far more worthy of preservation than any other spot connected with His earthly course. None other could have witnessed so many of His words and works. To no other could His disciples have returned with such fond and familiar recollections, as that where they first became acquainted with Him, and which had witnessed the greater part of their intercourse with Him. Yet it is this which has passed away, without even a memorial or tradition to mark its place." While the site of Capernaum is still a matter of dispute, it may be regarded as certain that it was somewhere on the plain or coast which borders the northwest section of the lake. A careful study of all the surface indications, in recent years, warrants the conclusion, to which all parties now give assent, that the limit of distance along this portion of the coast plain, in which the site of Capernaum is likely to be found, does not exceed a stretch of three miles. Within this limited territory there are two locations whose respective claims have been ably advocated by eminent writers and explorers. One, at the northeast corner of the Plain of Gennesaret, is marked by a ruined caravansary called Khan Minyeh, which has been known as a halting place on the road to Damascus for 700 years; the other location is about half way between Khan Minyeh and the inlet of the Jordan River, and is called Tell Hum. Its distance from Khan Minyeh is about two and a half miles. At Tell Hum there are extensive ruins, among which huge blocks of black basalt and delicately carved columns of marble, or fine white limestone, are indiscriminately mingled together. At one point a heap of columns, cornices, entablatures and sculptured slabs mark the site of a Jewish synagogue which was seventy-five feet in length and fifty-six feet in width. The suggestion that this synagogue was identical with the building in which Jesus taught while a resident of Capernaum has met with much favor among Bible students, and has contributed not a little to the support of the view that Tell Hum occupies the site of Capernaum. "If Tell Hum be Capernaum," says Colonel Wilson, "this is, without a doubt, the synagogue built by the Roman centurion, and one of the most sacred places on earth." To this supposition, however, there are some serious objections which may be briefly stated as follows:

(1) The name, which is supposed to be a modified form of Capernaum, does not furnish satisfactory evidence of its connection with the city of Capernaum. The similarity between the two words is apparent in the last syllable only. Dr. George Adams Smith makes the assertion that Tell Hum is an impossible contraction from Kephar-Nahum, and other eminent authorities regard it as at least a very unlikely supposition that Kephar, or Caper, which represents the Hebrew word for village, should be supplanted by the Arabic word Tell, inasmuch as there is no Tell or mound at the place. (2) The extensive ruins above ground at this place, including the synagogue, do not furnish any positive proof of

its connection with Capernaum. They might with equal propriety be regarded as the ruins of Chorazin, a city of like character and importance. It should be noted in this connection that nine synagogues, corresponding to the one at Tell Hum in their general features, have been found amid other ruins around the lake or on the hills of Galilee: and that most, if not all of them, are assigned by good authorities, to the period of the Jewish revival in the second century of our era. (3) Tell Hum is at least two miles from the great highway which leads to the north, and it seems likely that the rugged pathway by which it is now reached was its only connection by land with the old Roman road, which leaves the Lake at Khan Minyeh. (4) There are no remains of a fort or garrison in or near Tell Hum and no trace of a fountain, such as Josephus describes, and to which he gives the name of Kapharnaum. This fountain he also associates with the tract— as is evident from his own description—which is now known as the Plain of Gennesaret. (5) This site is outside the land of Gennesaret, in which we have every reason to believe the city of Capernaum was located. Canon Tristram, who is inclined to favor the site of Tell Hum, on other grounds, frankly says that "its distance from the Round Fountain and from the Plain of Gennesaret seems the obstacle to a decisive admission of its being the city of the Gospels." (6) There are no indications of a harbor at Tell Hum. After a careful examination Dr. Tristram came to the conclusion that "there are no traces of a harbor, and that it could never have been a convenient spot for fishing boats." This alone is a very formidable objection.

The advocates of this site are Colonel Wilson, Dr. W. M. Thomson, Renan, Ritter, and other eminent writers and explorers. The principal advocates of the site at Khan Minyeh are Dr. Edward Robinson, Merrill, Conder, Porter, Kitchener, Macgregor, Lightfoot and Keim.

The existence of a city at Khan Minyeh is indicated by a series of low mounds, which lie to the south of the khan, about one hundred yards from the seashore. The ruins above ground are not extensive as at Tell Hum, but hewn stones and strongly built limestone walls have been found at a depth of four or five feet. All the indications point to a buried city consigned to utter destruction in accordance with the sentence long ago pronounced against it. In front of this ruined site is the curved line of its ancient harbor and the beautiful strand fringed by a mass of luxuriant vegetation, and white with myriads of closely compacted fresh-water shells. A fountain called Ain et Tin bursts out from the foot of a cliff near the khan and runs directly into the lake. At its mouth is a marsh in which may still be seen a luxuriant growth of reeds and papyrus. This is the only place on the Lake of Galilee where the Egyptian papyrus is found, but at Lake Huleh it covers acres of the adjacent swampland. In the face of the cliff or bluff there is a wide trench, now used as a horse path, which was evidently hewn out of the rock with a view to carrying water to the plain from the fountain of Tabighah, about three-quarters of a mile distant. Dr. Merrill mentions the fact that many of the stones used in the construction of this aqueduct are found with the cement still adhering to them. The cutting in the rock, according to his measurement, is fifty-three feet above the surface of the lake.

Accepting the theory that the fountain to which Josephus refers was at Tabighah, Kitchener says: "The water was brought past Minyeh to the plain and was naturally called after that place. It could hardly be called after Tell Hum, a mile and three-quarters distant from the spring, and in the opposite direction." On the top of the hill in which the cutting is made there is an artificially levelled plateau with traces of walls and buildings, and also of steps leading up to it. The castle or garrison in which the centurion resided was probably on this height, while the custom-house would be at the point where the road from the north touches the lake.

Here then is a site which accords with the incidental accounts given by Josephus; with all the known facts relating to the city; with all the features which are lacking in the site farther to the north; and with all the incidents mentioned by the evangelist in the gospel narrative. It connects the home of Jesus with the most beautiful spot on the Lake of Galilee; with a natural

ROCK CLIFF AND FOUNTAIN (AIN ET TIN) AT KHAN MINYEH.
The Papyrus grows luxuriantly on the marsh which borders the Lake.

harbor, where the boats of the fishermen could glide up smoothly and safely to the shore; with a long shelly beach firm and hard as a floor; and with a plain unequalled for fertility in all the world.

IX

BETHSAIDA OF GALILEE

The theory that there were originally two places called Bethsaida on the Sea of Galilee—one of which was on the western shore—has been disputed by some noted writers and explorers, but the evidence in its favor rests upon well authenticated facts of observation and history.

In dealing with this contention it should be noted at the outset, that the officially recognized boundary line between the Roman province of Galilee and Gaulanitis was the Upper Jordan and the eastern border of the Sea of Galilee.

During the period of our Lord's public ministry these provinces were ruled by Herod Antipas and Herod Philip. The eastern shore was for the most part a desert or uninhabited region, but on the western shore cities and villages were thickly clustered together. It is worthy of note in this connection, also, that from time immemorial it has been the custom to speak of the country eastward of the Jordan and its lakes as "the other side"; and the same phraseology has been used to indicate the western shore by those who lived or journeyed, on the eastern side. In this sense the evangelists always use the term, or its equivalent expressions, as the parallel passages and incidental references clearly show. (Compare

Matt. 8: 28; Mark 5: 1; Luke 8: 26, with Matt. 9: 1; Mark 5: 21; Luke 8: 40; also, Luke 9: 10, 11; John 6: 1, 2, with Matt. 14: 22; Mark 6: 45; John 6: 22, 23 and 53.)

There is no controversy with respect to the existence of a town originally called Bethsaida on the eastern side of the Upper Jordan. While its exact position is not definitely known, it is certain that it was in the district of Gaulanitis and not far from the spot where the river entered the lake. Josephus says that Philip "advanced the village Bethsaida, situate at the Lake of Gennesareth, unto the dignity of a city, both by the number of inhabitants it contained, and its other grandeur, and called it by the name of Julias, the same name with Cæsar's daughter" (Antiq. XVIII, 2, 1).

In other passages the Jewish historian indicates its position as "beyond Jordan"; in "lower Gaulanitis": and as being "alongside the river, which flowed past it into the lake."

In every instance, however, except the one above noted, he calls it *Julias* (Wars II, 8, 1 and 13, 2; Antiq. II, 9, 1; Wars III, 12, 7; Life, 72). Pliny mentions the city of Julias, also, and places it on the east side of the lake. The modern designation Bethsaida-Julias, is not to be found in ancient history, sacred or secular. Luke calls it Bethsaida, its original designation according to Josephus, but all other writers of the Roman period drop the old name and invariably call it Julias.

The only site which seems to accord with the descriptions of this royal city of Philip, is a mound or knoll, partly covered with ruins, in the northwest corner of the plain of Batihah. This site, known as Et Tell, is close to the principal fording place of the Jordan on the plain, but it is more than a mile and a half from the north end of the lake. Local changes in the river delta may have increased the distance between these points since the time of Christ, but if Et Tell represents the site of Julias, it must always have been a considerable distance from the head of the lake. It is not unlikely, however—as Dr. Merrill suggests—that the landing place of Julias was the original site of the town, and that among the local fishermen it retained its old name for some time after the building of the city of Philip, which would naturally be laid out on higher ground. "A fishing place, a Bethsaida—as he expresses it—must of necessity be on the lake. After the city was built away from it, a fishing place would still remain. . . . Fishermen would resort thither, and passengers and merchandise for Julias would be landed there. But it was a small place, it had no synagogue, and to the Jews was a village." This explanation accords with the statement in Mark's Gospel (8: 22–26), where the same Bethsaida, as the context indicates, is described as a *village* (see verses 10 and 13). Near this place a blind man was healed, but there is no intimation that Jesus, whose mission was to the lost sheep of the house of Israel, ever entered the Græco-

Roman cities of Tiberias and Julias in which Herod Antipas and Herod Philip held court.

The scene of the miraculous feeding of the multitude, mention of which is made by all of the evangelists, was evidently on the eastern edge of the Batihah plain, in the immediate vicinity of the lake. This place fulfills all the conditions of the several narratives. It is recognized by Luke as belonging to the District of Bethsaida and yet it was a region apart from the towns, where the native grass thickly covered the fallow ground and made a comfortable resting-place for the weary multitudes. To this retreat Jesus came by ship from some point on the northwestern side of the sea for rest and seclusion; but the people, we are told, ran afoot out of all the cities, when they had noted the direction in which Jesus sailed, and, reaching the other side before the vessel arrived, were ready to meet Him at the landing place. Moved with pity towards this vast concourse of people, who were as sheep not having a shepherd, Jesus ascended a gentle slope at the foot of the adjacent mountain; and, as the people gathered closely around Him, "began to teach them many things of the kingdom of God, and heal them that had need of healing." When the day began to wear away He again manifested His compassion as well as His almighty power by multiplying the five loaves and two fishes, which were brought to Him by the disciples, for the supply of their immediate temporal needs.

In view of these facts it is admitted without

hesitation that two of the passages in which Bethsaida is mentioned by the evangelists refer to the place, on the eastern side of the Jordan, whose claims we have been considering. It seems impossible, however, to refer the five remaining references to this site without impugning the accuracy of the Gospel narratives. It has been intimated by some writers that the existence of a second Bethsaida was *invented* to meet a supposed difficulty in the narratives of the evangelists, but this is not a fair statement of the case. A second Bethsaida, belonging to the province of Galilee, is designated by name as well as implied by incidental reference. Its claims are advocated mainly, if not solely, on the ground that it is *in* the *record*.

The main points of the argument in favor of a western Bethsaida may be briefly summed up as follows:

1. In the narrative of the return journey, after the miraculous feeding of the multitude, it is distinctly stated that the disciples embarked in a ship "to go to the *other side* before unto Bethsaida," while Jesus sent the multitudes away (Mark 6: 45). If the words "unto or towards Bethsaida" stood alone, there might be some ground for the supposition that the disciples aimed to sail along the shore towards Bethsaida-Julias, but in the description which follows, the evangelist makes it plain that the "other side," as he uses the expression, means the western shore of the lake: "And *when they had passed*

BETHSAIDA OF GALILEE.
(Ain Tabighah.)

over they came into the land of Gennesaret" (6: 33). The parallel accounts convey the same impression and are equally decisive on this point: "Jesus straightway constrained His disciples to get into a ship, says Matthew, and to go before Him *unto the other side.*" "And *when they were gone over* they came into the land of Gennesaret" (14: 22 and 34). John says: "And when even was now come His disciples went down unto the sea, and entered into a ship, and *went over the sea towards Capernaum*" (6: 16, 17). There is no discrepancy between the statements of Mark and John, if Dr. Robinson is right in identifying Et Tabighah with Bethsaida. The general direction would be the same, and the distance between the two points does not exceed three-quarters of a mile. During the night the disciples made little progress because the wind was *contrary*, but in the dawning of the morning Jesus appeared to them walking on the sea. Afterwards they received Him into the ship; "and immediately the ship was at the land *whither they went*" (John 6: 21). In keeping with these statements is the mention of the fact that "the multitude which stood on the other side of the sea, and noted the direction taken by the vessel in which the disciples sailed, took shipping the following day and came to Capernaum, seeking for Jesus" (John 6: 22-24). These passages, interpreted in their natural and ordinary sense, clearly show that the disciples aimed to go to the western side of the lake, in obedience to the command of Jesus. The contrary wind *retarded* their progress, but it did not take them far out of their course. The undisputed mention of Bethsaida in this connection with Capernaum makes it highly probable, also, that its site was somewhere in the same neighborhood.

2. This testimony is verified and corroborated by the association of Bethsaida with Capernaum and Chorazin in the judgment pronounced by our Lord upon these highly favored cities, "Woe unto thee, Chorazin! woe unto thee, Bethsaida! for if the mighty works, which were done in you, had been done in Tyre and Sidon, they would have repented long ago in sack-cloth and ashes. And thou Capernaum, which art exalted unto heaven, shalt be brought down to hell" (Matt. 11: 21–23). There is no uncertainty with respect to the import of this denunciation. It does not apply to a gentile, or foreign, city, like Julias, for it is here *contrasted* with the gentile cities of Tyre and Sidon. It is evident, also, that its significance inheres in the declaration that this city shared with Capernaum and Chorazin of Galilee, in peculiar privileges and oft-repeated manifestations of supernatural power in connection with the ministry of Jesus. In other words, it was in the very centre of that field of wonders honored above all other places as the residence of Jesus to which multitudes flocked from every quarter of the land. This region, as we know from many direct and incidental notices, was within the domain ruled by Herod

Antipas, extending from Magdala on the coast to the inlet of the Jordan. We have the record of three brief visits of our Lord to the half-heathen population on the other side of the lake, mainly for rest and retirement, but there is no record of "many mighty works" in connection with any of the towns or cities of the eastern shore. We read of itineraries within the coast of Tiberias and Julias—as within the coasts of Tyre and Sidon—but there is no record that Jesus ever entered either of these Herodian cities. This of itself seems to be an unanswerable argument against the proposed identification of the city, to which Jesus refers in this passage, with Julias in the district of Gaulanitis.

3. The testimony of the Evangelist John is still more definite and explicit. In one passage he tells us that Philip—one of the apostolic band—was of Bethsaida, the city of Andrew and Peter (John 1: 45). In another place (12: 20) he gives the further information that Philip was of Bethsaida of Galilee. This testimony, as Dr. Merrill puts it, has but one meaning; namely, Bethsaida was a well-known place, it was in Galilee, and it was a "city" (polis). Those who assume that there was only one Bethsaida, and that it was on the east side of the lake, must either discredit or explain away these plain matter-of-fact statements. They are made by one who is eminently worthy of respect and confidence; who knew every foot of this lakeside region, and who, in common with the other

evangelists, always speaks of these associates as near neighbors and as *men of Galilee*. We can hardly regard it as among the possibilities that the apostle John, himself a Galilean, and probably of the same place, should deliberately make the statement that this city was in Galilee, if it were actually a part of the territory of Herod Philip, or on the other side of the river or lake. The fact that he mentions Galilee at all in this connection is a strong presumptive proof that he wished to distinguish it from the other Bethsaida on the eastern side. Cana of Galilee is a similar expression in the same gospel. Dr. George A. Smith attempts to reconcile the evangelist's statement with his theory that there was only one Bethsaida, on the assumption that the province of Galilee included "most of the level coastland east of the lake." This is an extraordinary assumption, if it applies to Galilee in the time of Christ, and is apparently in conflict with all the evidence which the history of that time has given us. In support of his opinion, Dr. Smith instances the single fact that Josephus sometimes calls Judas of Gamala a Galilean. It does not follow, however, that Josephus means by this that Gamala was a city belonging to the *province of Galilee*. This designation might have been used to indicate that Judas was *born* on the western side of the lake: or it may have been given to him in an indefinite sense, because he was at the head of an insurrection, which had its rise in Galilee. However this may be, the same author tells us that Judas was *a Gaulanite* of a city whose name was Gamala (Antiq. 18: 1, 1); and also, by implication, that Julias and Gamala were regarded as outside of Galilee in his day (Life, 71).

The objection sometimes urged that the existence of two towns of the same name in close neighborhood is improbable, has little weight in view of the fact that these towns were in different provinces, under different rulers, and in many respects had but little in common. The name itself suggests a place favorably situated for fishermen, and might with propriety be applied to more places than one by the seashore.

Dr. Thomson suggests the possibility of a Bethsaida on either bank of the Jordan, and indicates a place near the mouth of the river—where some ruins have been found—as the probable location of the Galilean city. This supposition accords with the affirmative view of this question, but the site itself does not accord with the history of the region, nor with the narratives of the evangelists.

The generally accepted site of Bethsaida of Galilee is Ain et Tabighah. It is at the head of a charming little bay on the northern side of the spur, which runs out into the sea at Kahn Minyeh. The conclusion reached by Dr. Robinson that Khan Minyeh represents Capernaum; Et Tabighah, Bethsaida; and Tell Hum, Chorazin, has had many able advocates in recent years and has been greatly strengthened by the results of careful research. "It may be a small thing," says Dr. Fish, "upon which to construct a theory, but certainly it is a fact of interest, that if these locations be accepted as the right ones, there is a beautiful *order* in Christ's enumeration of the three cities named. And we can fancy Him uttering, with the finger pointing towards each in succession, down along the lake, the denunciation upon Chorazin, Bethsaida, Capernaum."

This view is strengthened by the account of Jerome and by the narrative of Willibald, who visited the Holy Land in the year 722. From Tiberias his party went round the sea and by the village of Magdala to Capernaum: and thence they went to Bethsaida and the next morning to Chorazin.

It only remains to be said that this location accords with all the direct and incidental notices given of Bethsaida of Galilee by the evangelists. It is near to Capernaum; it has a safe harbor; a good anchorage; a beach rising rapidly where boats can safely approach the shore; a coast free from débris and driftwood; and in this vicinity the fish are more plentiful than at any other point on the lake shore. It is still a "Fishertown" where boats are landed, where nets are dried and fish are sorted for the market, as in the days of Philip and Andrew and Peter.

X

THE MOUNTAIN OF THE TRANSFIGURATION

THERE are three mountains which have been hallowed, and made forever memorable in the history of Redemption, by supereminent manifestations of the Divine glory.

One is Mount Sinai upon which the glory of the Lord rested for many days, "and the sight of this glory was like devouring fire on the top of the mount in the eyes of the children of Israel:" another is Mount Zion, "the mountain of the heights of Israel"—"the holy mountain of God,"—on which the Shekinah rested as the visible manifestation of the abiding presence of Jehovah: the third is "the high mountain," which Peter designates as "the holy mount," where Jesus was transfigured before His chosen disciples, "and His face did shine as the sun, and His raiment was white as the light."

The mountain of the Transfiguration is not mentioned by name in the narrative of the evangelists, and the only clue to its location is in the incidental notices which connect it with our Lord's brief sojourn in the neighborhood of Cesarea Philippi. A monastic tradition as old as the fourth century, in apparent disregard of these incidental notices, has located the scene of the

Transfiguration on Mount Tabor in Galilee. During the sixth century three churches were built upon the summit of Tabor to commemorate this event, and from that date until the beginning of the latter half of the present century this traditional assumption has been generally accepted by biblical scholars. Mount Tabor is a conspicuous elevation of rare beauty and symmetry in its outlines and proportions, and has been aptly styled the Righi of this mountain region. There is no intimation, however, in the sacred narrative which in anywise connects it with the scene of this great Epiphany. It has frequent mention in the Old Testament as a famous landmark and rallying point in Israel, but there is not a single allusion to it, either by name or association, in the New Testament. Apart from this negative evidence there are two good reasons for the rejection of the tradition which locates the Transfiguration on Mount Tabor.

(1) At the date of this occurrence Tabor was in the midst of a dense population. A great highway from the plateau above led past its base, and a fortified city occupied permanently by a Roman garrison, crowned its summit. Amid such surroundings it would have been difficult, if not impossible, to find a quiet retreat for uninterrupted communion and prayer, such as the narrative implies.

(2) In this narrative the Transfiguration is closely associated with a group of events which unquestionably took place on or about the south-

ern slope of Mount Hermon. The most notable of these are the confession of Peter and the prophetic declaration of Jesus, immediately following it, concerning His approaching sufferings and death. "After these sayings"—as Luke puts it—"Jesus took Peter and John and James, and went *up into the mountain* (to 'oros) to pray." Of the six full days which followed "these sayings" there is no record, but it is in keeping with the purport of the entire narrative to assume that they were spent in meditation and retirement. The Transfiguration is the answer to the doubts and questionings of the dismayed disciples, and there is no intimation that the Master passed the momentous hours of this transition period in travel, or that He sought another place, amid the thickly settled population of Galilee, for this crowning manifestation of His Divinity and Messiahship: on the contrary, it is asserted in Mark's gospel (9: 30) that Christ passed through Galilee *after* He had healed the spirit-possessed child at the foot of the mountain. This is the mountain on which He was transfigured, and the language certainly implies that it was outside the Galilean bounds. This would be literally true of the coasts of Cesarea Philippi, which were a part of the district of Gaulanitis, governed by Herod Philip.

The argument in favor of Mount Hermon has been happily set forth by John Ruskin in his famous essay on "Mountains." "All the immediately preceding ministries of Christ"—he says

—"had been at Cæsarea Philippi. There is no mention of travel southward in the six days that intervened between the warning given to His disciples, and the going up into the hill. What other hill could it be than the southward slope of that goodly mountain, Hermon, which is indeed the centre of all the Promised Land, from the entering in of Hamath unto the river of Egypt; the mount of fruitfulness, from which the springs of Jordan descended to the valleys of Israel. Along its mighty forest avenues, until the grass grew fair with the mountain lilies, His feet dashed in the dew of Hermon, He must have gone to pray His first recorded prayer about death; and from the steep of it, before He knelt, could see to the south all the dwelling-places of the people that had sat in darkness, and seen the great light, the land of Zabulon and of Naphtali, Galilee of the nations;—could see, even with His human sight, the gleam of the lake by Capernaum and Chorazin, and many a place loved by Him, and vainly ministered to, whose house was now left unto them desolate; and, chief of all, far in the utmost blue, the hills above Nazareth, sloping down to His old home: hills on which yet the stones lay loose, that had been taken up to cast at Him, when He left them forever."

Mount Hermon trends farther to the west than the main ridge of the Anti-Lebanon range. It is almost separated from it and towers high above it. Its elevation above the level of the sea is

9,383 feet. It is buttressed by ridges of lesser elevation, so compactly grouped around it that it seems to rise, as one gigantic mass, almost directly from the plains or lower levels that skirt its base. The noble contour of its glittering dome may be seen from the lowest reaches of the Jordan valley; from the shores of the Sea of Galilee; from the Huleh basin; and from almost every elevated plain, and mountain in Eastern and Western Palestine. As seen from the south Hermon stands, with snowy summit reaching to the clouds, apparently at the head of the great cleft between the mountain ranges. From the east the view is more comprehensive and scarcely less imposing and majestic. As ordinarily seen by travellers to the East, the lofty heights of Mount Hermon are covered with a glittering mantle of ice and snow. On the twentieth of March we found snowdrifts so deep as to be almost impassable, on the road to Damascus over the shoulder of Hermon, at an elevation of less than 5,000 feet. The crystal streams which issue from this mass of slowly-melting snow pour out from the base of the mountain from the south and west, going down by the valleys, and through each successive level of the descending course of the Jordan to the deep basin of the Dead Sea. The fountain of Banias, the most picturesque source of the Jordan, springs directly from the southern base of Mount Hermon. There is no place in Palestine—and there are but few places perhaps in all the world—

where so many elements of grandeur and beauty are grouped together in happy combination.

The prominent features of this Syrian Tivoli,— as Dean Stanley terms it—are a broad terrace clothed with luxurious vegetation "all alive with streams of water and cascades;" a precipitous cliff at the mountain's foot something more than 100 feet high; the remains of ruined temples; and, at the bottom of the cliff, a cave whose mouth is partly closed with loose stones which have fallen from the roof, or from the summit of the cliff. Out of this mass of boulders and débris, and apparently from crevices between the strata of the rock alongside, a foam-crested stream bursts forth, "a full born river, along a line of thirty feet." A short distance from its source this flood of seething waters is collected together in a large pool, and thence becomes a swift torrent, roaring and dashing over the rocks, and gliding amid dense thickets of oleander, hawthorn and cane, until it is lost to view in the depths of a dark ravine.

The site of the ancient city which grew up around this "sanctuary of waters" can still be traced by its ruins, most of which belong to the Roman period. Near the fountain Herod the Great built a temple of white marble in honor of Augustus. At a later period the city was rebuilt and adorned with palaces, temples, and villas by Philip the Tetrarch, who named it Cæsarea Philippi. The modern name Banias is the equiv-

SOURCE OF THE JORDAN AT BANIAS.
This fountain—the most picturesque source of the Jordan—issues from the southern base of Mt. Hermon "in the coasts of Caesarea Philippi" (Matt. 16:14).

alent of the old Greek name Paneas—the abode of the sylvan god Pan.

Into this restful region abounding in quiet nooks and unbroken solitudes,—the borderland between Jew and Gentile—the Master came with His disciples for a definite purpose. The burden of every wayside conversation, of every prophetic utterance, of every Divine manifestation on this eventful journey was the Decease, or Exodus, which He should accomplish at Jerusalem. With this thought pressing heavily upon Him, as the crisis drew near, Jesus dismissed the multitudes which thronged Him in Galilee, crossed over the lake to the eastern side, and thence journeyed northward some thirty miles to the place within the coasts of Cæsarea Philippi—not definitely mentioned by the evangelists—where the events preceding the Transfiguration took place. Here, as we have seen, Jesus unfolded the nature of His redemptive work; prepared the minds of the disciples for the sore disappointments and fiery trials which were awaiting them; elicited the brief, but all-comprehensive confession of Simon Peter; and gave assurance, in language of unmistakable import, of the permanence and ultimate triumph of His Church, amid all its dangers and over all its adversaries.

After these things Jesus took the three chosen disciples and went up into the mountain to pray; "and as He prayed the fashion of His countenance was altered, and His raiment was white and glistening. And behold, there talked with

Him two men, which were Moses and Elias who appeared in glory, and spake of His decease which He should accomplish at Jerusalem." "He was transfigured," says Mark, "before them, and His garments became exceeding white as no fuller on earth can white them." "His face did shine as the sun," says Matthew, "and His raiment was white as the light." Here the radiant form, the shining garments, the attendant representatives of the Law and the Prophets from the unseen world, the bright overshadowing cloud, and the voice out of the cloud—each in turn testified of Him whom God the Father had sent into the world to be the propitiation for our sins. The light which shone upon this Holy Mount—a light such as "never was on sea or land"—was a glimpse of the glory which shineth evermore in the home-land of Jesus, where they need no candle neither light of the sun; a foregleam of the glory which should attend the Exodus, not of our Lord only, but of all those who have passed from death unto life through faith in His name. Long after these events the Apostle Peter makes use of this mountain vision to inspire the hope and strengthen the confidence of his fellow-Christians. "We have not followed cunningly devised fables,"—he writes—" when we made known unto you the power and coming of our Lord Jesus Christ, but were eye-witnesses of His Majesty. For He received from God the Father honor and glory, when there came such a voice to Him from the excellent glory, This is My beloved Son, in whom I am well pleased. And this voice which came from Heaven we heard, when we were with Him in the holy mount."

XI

THE PLACE OF "THE NOBLE SANCTUARY"

FROM the summit of the Mount of Olives every object in and about Jerusalem comes within the range of easy vision and stands out, as on a relief map, with startling distinctness. The most conspicuous feature within the limits of this panoramic view is the sacred enclosure in which, beyond all question, once stood the successive Temples of Solomon, Zerubbabel and Herod. The massive walls which surround it rise at some points to the height of seventy and eighty feet, and the space thus enclosed contains an area of nearly thirty-five acres. Its extent from north to south is more than 1,500 feet, or nearly one-third of a mile. From east to west it measures about 1,000 feet. In outline the enclosure is an irregular quadrangle formed by cutting away huge masses of rock at some points, filling in valleys and depressions at others, and by building up immense substructions, retaining walls and supporting vaults where the ground fell away too rapidly to admit of filling up with loose stone and rubbish. Except the raised platform in the centre, which covers an area of five acres and is paved with slabs of limestone and marble, the surface is for the most part an unincumbered

THE MOSQUE OF EL AKSA—TEMPLE AREA.

greensward dotted here and there with cyprus and olive-trees. In the early spring-time this vacant space is covered with the short native grass which grows on the hills around it and is spangled with wild flowers of rare delicacy of form and richness of color.

Those who are privileged to enter this secluded spot pass in a moment from the confusion and discomforts of the narrow streets and the jostling crowds into a charming retreat, where, for the nonce, all distracting sights and sounds are shut out, and where amid the hush of holy memories the ordinary cares of life are all forgotten.

This is the one sacred place in Jerusalem which is revered alike by Moslems, Christians and Jews. In the plain, matter-of-fact descriptions of modern writers and explorers it is usually designated as the "Temple Area," but throughout the Arabic-speaking world, where poetry dominates in nomenclature, as well as in description and story, it is known as the Haram esh Sherif,—the Place of the "Noble Sanctuary." Than this no designation could be more felicitous or appropriate. It accords with all that we know of the magnificent structure which once crowned this mountain height and extended in terraced platforms down its sides.

The oldest of the buildings that now occupy this sacred site is the Great Mosque of El Aksa. It is directly south of the raised platform and extends to the outer wall of the Haram. With its associated buildings it covers a space 272 feet long by 184 wide. The original structure, which like the mosque of St. Sophia, at Constantinople was once a Christian church, was built by the Emperor Justinian in the fourth century. It had a grand nave supported by columns and arches with three aisles of corresponding proportions and was regarded as one of the largest and finest Basilicas in Christendom.

The Dome of the Rock (Kubbet es Sakhra), which "next after Mecca is the most sacred, and next after Cordova the most beautiful of Moslem shrines" occupies the centre of the raised platform; around it are grouped several smaller buildings and praying places, fashioned in excellent taste and decorated with rich carvings in wood and marble.

"Taking it in mass and detail," says Hepworth Dixon, "this group on the Temple hill,—the mosques of Omar and Aksa, the domes, the terraces, the colonnades, the kiosks and fountains—is perhaps the very noblest specimen of building art in Asia."

The lower portion of the Dome of the Rock is a regular octagon, the side being sixty-seven feet. The central or raised portion which rests upon the octagon is circular and over this rises an exquisitely poised and proportioned dome surmounted by a gilt crescent. The circlet below the dome and the upper portion of the octagon are overlaid with oriental tiles in delicately tinted colors, bordered with Arabesque ornaments and Arabic inscriptions. The lower or basement portion of the octagon is cased with slabs of rich variegated marble. The height of the building, including the marble platform upon which it rests, is 170 feet.

The interior is admirably proportioned, the diameter being 150 feet. It is richly decorated with costly marbles, inlaid tiles and gilded mosaics. Interwoven with these are Arabic inscriptions in gilt from the Koran. Indications of mosaic work outside the building have also been found in places; and it is possible—as some of the early writers assert—that the upper portion of the octagon was originally adorned with mosaics on the outside, as well as in the interior.

The windows of stained glass in and above the octagon are unequalled for beauty of pattern and intense, glowing colors, unless it be by the famous windows, which modern art cannot reproduce, in some of the mosques in Constantinople.

Four great doors,—one at each cardinal point of the compass—open into an encircling corridor, thirteen feet wide. This corridor, or octagonal isle, is separated from an inner aisle of similar character, thirty feet in width, by a screen consisting of eight piers and sixteen columns of marble and granite.

The Sakhra, or sacred rock, which rises four feet nine and a half inches above the marble floor, at its highest point, occupies the centre of the building, directly under the great dome. It is encircled by an inner course, or screen, consisting of four massive piers and twelve columns. The arches which rest upon these piers support the dome. If the platform upon which the entire structure rests were removed the rock would stand fifteen feet above the level of the Temple area. As it now appears it is a mass or ledge of rough gray limestone fifty-seven feet long and forty-three feet wide. A canopy of gracefully disposed crimson silk overhangs it, and an iron railing surmounted by arrow-heads guards it from profane handling.

Whatever may be said with respect to its position within the Temple, or its courts, the Sakhra is unquestionably the summit or central peak of Mount Moriah.

Under an archway at the southeast side of the rock a flight of eleven steps leads down to an artificial cave which has a superficial area of about 600 feet.

Its average height is six or seven feet. In its original condition it was a rock-hewn chamber, or cistern, whose only opening was through a hole, now utilized as a window, in the overarching roof. A circular slab in the floor covers the entrance to a shaft or lower chamber, which the Moslems call the "Well of Souls." The existence of this hollow space can readily be ascertained by tapping upon the stone, but the custodians of the Sacred Rock have long and persistently refused to permit the removal of the slab, with a view to an examination of the cavity or its connections. No light has been thrown

THE DOME OF THE ROCK AND ITS ASSOCIATED BUILDINGS.
Platform of the Temple Area.

upon this mysterious passageway to lower depths in the rock by Christian writers during the period of its occupancy by the Crusaders, and up to this date the Moslem spirits, which are said to inhabit it, have kept the secret of its original purpose and connections to themselves. It is asserted in the Rabbinical writings that the blood and refuse of the daily sacrifices within the Temple court were carried off by an underground channel to the valley of Hinnom, and it is possible that this basin in the rock, which could easily be flushed with the abundant water supply of the Temple, was connected with shafts and conduits leading down under the bed of the Tyropœan Valley to the place of burning in the great valley below.

However this may be it is certain that covered drains leading in this direction were constructed at an early period, the remains of which have been found beneath the triple gate and under a paved road down the Tyropœan Valley. In the former case, at least the obvious purpose was to carry off the wastage and overflow from the water supply of the Temple area.

Between the dome of the rock and the mosque of El Aksa the underlying rock is literally honeycombed with cisterns and reservoirs of much more than ordinary capacity. These rock-hewn tanks, numbering more than thirty in the survey chart, were connected together by channels and conduits and it is estimated that the total storage capacity of the series was about 12,000,000 gallons. One of these reservoirs, known as the "Great Sea," has a capacity of 2,000,000 gallons. The principal source of the water supply for the Temple and its courts was the Pools of Solomon fed by the clear, sparkling water which for centuries has flowed continuously from the "Sealed Fountain," a few rods from the upper pool. This never-failing spring is nine miles south of Jerusalem, but the course followed by the aqueduct was about fourteen miles. The high level aqueduct tapped a source of supply farther to the south. The main object of its construction seems to have been the supply of the upper city on the west side of the Tyropœan Valley.

It is a noteworthy fact in this connection that the Turkish government has recently constructed a pipe line, connecting with the low level aqueduct at Bethlehem, which now brings water from the "Sealed Fountain" above Solomon's Pools to the Temple area.

To the extent of its capacity,—which is very limited in comparison with the ancient aqueduct,—Jerusalem is once more supplied with pure water from the mountains as in the days of Solomon and Herod.

The inauguration ceremony in honor of this event took place on the 27th of November, 1901, when the water was turned on from the main pipe in the Haram esh-Sherif in the presence of the Governor and other distinguished guests.

The walls which enclose the "Place of the

Noble Sanctuary" represent the work of many distinct periods in the long and eventful history of the Holy City. At several points in the upper courses, and especially along the line of the north wall there are unmistakable indications of modern constructions from materials which had been used by former builders. Amid these changes and reconstructions there are abundant evidences, however, all along the line of the Haram wall, of the engineering skill and solid workmanship of the builders of the Herodian age. Back of this also, but not so easily accessible, are the courses of great stones, such as Warren found, nearly a hundred feet below the ground, with the marking of red paint which the Phœnician stone squarers had put upon them when they laid the foundations of the great enclosing wall in the days of Solomon. These indications of ancient workmanship have been found at the northeast corner of the Haram, where there is an accumulation of débris of 125 feet; and at the southeast corner where the accumulation exceeds eighty feet. At the latter point, therefore, the wall, if cleared to its lowest course, would be over 150 feet in height, while at the former it would be still higher.

In the lower courses of the east, south and west walls several of the stones exceed twenty feet in length, and are from six to eight feet in depth. Near the southeast corner there is a single stone twenty-six feet in length, whose estimated weight is over one hundred tons: another in the south wall measures thirty-eight feet nine inches in length.

"By the repeated sinking of shafts on the sloping face of Ophel," says Dr. Tristram, "it is established that the south wall is buried more than half its depth beneath an accumulation of rubbish, and that, if bared to its foundation, this wall would present an unbroken front of masonry, of nearly 1,000 feet long and 150 feet in height. The wall, as it now stands, with less than half that height emerging from the ground, has always been regarded as a marvel. What must it have been when entirely exposed to view, and the tall erections of the Temple towering over it."

Of the Roman period the most notable remains are the scarped rock-wall and rock-hewn trench connected with the Tower of Antonia, on the north side of the Haram; the Double, or Huldah gate in the south wall, with its inner vestibule and the vaulted passageway leading up to the cloisters of the Temple court: the conduit which supplied the Temple with water—a probable reparation of the older water course in use during the period of the first temple;—the fragmentary remains of arches springing from the west wall, —known as Robinson's and Wilson's arches,— representing two noble viaducts which spanned the Tyropœan Valley; and the several gateways and vaulted passages which lead up from this side to the western cloisters of the Temple. There is a difference of opinion with respect to the antiquity of the Golden Gate in the east wall, but the best authorities regard it as an addition of the later Roman period. A line drawn directly west from this gate, or a point a little north of it, would probably mark the northern limit of the extension of the court of Herod's Temple. Beyond this, on the west side, there was a valley formerly about thirty feet deep, which was partially filled up by Pompey when he assaulted the defenses of the Temple, in the year 65 B. C.

The stronghold of Antonia, which towered high above the enclosing wall and dominated the Temple courts, was built upon a ledge of native rock in the northwest corner of the Haram.

It is a significant fact that within the limits of the Haram walls, as they now stand, there is not a trace or fragment, either of outline or structure of the Temple or its courts, except the Sakhra under the Dome of the Rock, and the small boundary stone, found by M. Ganneau, upon which may still be read the inscription in large Greek characters, which warned the uncircumcised stranger not to pass the limits of the Gentile Court.

The great walls which remain to-day are only the walls of the *Temple Area.* They *enclosed* the Sanctuary, but they did not form a part of it. Of this great structure, to its outmost bound of court and cloister, it is literally true, as our Lord predicted, that "there has not been left here one stone upon another, that has not been thrown down" (Matt. 24: 2). Because of this total destruction the exact site of the Holy House and the Great Altar which stood in front of it is still a matter of uncertainty and of earnest discussion. It should be noted also that the entrances, to which reference has been made, were subterranean passages leading up to the real gates of the Temple on higher levels, within the great enclosing wall.

The general plan of the second Temple, as reconstructed by Herod the Great, corresponded exactly with the original Temple of Solomon, with the exception of the enlargement outside the consecrated limits of the "Mountain of the House." This enlargement, upon which Herod expended vast sums of money in order, if possible, to rival the glory of the Sanctuary, from which he himself was excluded by the "law of the House," was known as the Outer or Gentile Court. This court, or lower platform, according to the estimate of Sir Charles Warren, was 900 feet in length on each side. Its breadth on the north side was 140 feet; on the east 180 feet; on the south 460 feet. On the west side the breadth cannot be given with certainty, inasmuch as the exact position of the altar of sacrifice is not definitely known. It may have been one hundred feet; or its outer limit may have been very near to the great enclosing (Haram) wall.

Next the outer wall on each side were cloisters or colonnades in double rows. The one on the east side was known as Solomon's Porch in the time of Christ. It had two aisles bordered by majestic columns of white marble and its pavement was a rare mosaic of costly stones. Below it was the Kidron Valley and over against it was the western slope of the Mount of Olives.

On the south side of this noble platform, which, as Josephus assures us, enlarged the area of the Temple to twice its former extent, was the Stoa Basilica, or Royal Porch, which greatly surpassed all the other cloisters in extent and beauty, and was regarded as the chief glory of the Outer Court. It was 105 feet in breadth and was divided into three spacious arcades. The one in the centre was one hundred feet in height and forty-five in breadth; the side arcades being fifty feet in height and thirty in breadth. "This cloister alone," says Professor Henderson, " was greater than York Minister or Westminster Abbey. The bridge which crossed the Tyropœan at Robinson's arch ran straight with the central colonnade. At the southeast corner the roof of the cloister was 326 feet above the bed of the Kidron. The height of the pinnacle, which is said to have risen at that corner is unknown; whatever it was, it must be added to that giddy height of 326 feet." The pillars of this portico, which like all the rest were solid marble of dazzling whiteness, numbered 162 and were each sixty feet in height. The floor like Solomon's Porch was paved with inlaid stones and the roofs covering the colonnades were of cedar from the forests of Lebanon.

The *inner* side of the Gentile Court was surrounded by a stone balustrade of elegant construction, five feet in height, which fenced off the Sacred Enclosure of the Israelites from the outside world. "Upon this wall," says Josephus, "stood pillars, at equal distances from one another, declaring the law of purity, some in Greek, and some in Roman letters: 'That no foreigner should go within that Sanctuary.'" The tablet or inscribed stone, found by M. Ganneau was one of these notices, and, as already intimated, it is the only authentic relic of the Temple itself which has yet been discovered.

This wall of partition between Gentile and Jew was called the *Soreg*. The several courts and buildings within it, rising to the very summit of the mountain, were known, collectively, as the *"Mountain of the House."* It was 500 cubits—or about 750 feet—square. The outer court of this sacred enclosure was called the *Chel*. It was a large, open space, apparently the same width on each side, with five entrance gates. In front of each gate was a flight of fourteen steps leading up from the Court of the Gentiles. On the inner side of the Chel, or terrace, rose a massive wall sixty feet or more in height. Every avenue of approach to this wall was strongly fortified, and its gateways, nine in number, were of great height and strength and, according to Josephus, " were covered over with gold and silver, as were the jambs of their doors and lintels." This structure as a whole was "a mighty citadel within a citadel." The open spaces or courts within this enclosure were on different levels in an ascending series, and were bordered on the outer sides by storerooms or cloisters; collectively they were known as the *Inner Court*. The first platform above the Outer Court, or Chel, was designated as "The Court of the Women." This was on the east side of the sacred enclosure. It was reached by a flight of twelve steps and was eight feet higher than the Chel. This court was an open space nearly 300 feet square, flanked on its north and south sides by large store chambers. Three large gateways, included in the number already mentioned, opened into it from the outside: one being in the north, another in the south and the third in the east. The eastern gate was one of the largest and most magnificent entrances to the Temple or its courts. It was on a line with the eastern gates of the Soreg, and occupied a commanding position in the forefront of the great Sanctuary. Its probable identification with the "Beautiful Gate" (Acts 3: 2) is generally conceded by those who have made a careful study of the descriptions of the Temple, as it appeared in the time of our Lord. It was made of fine Corinthian brass, and it is said that it required the strength of twenty men to open and close its doors. Josephus tells us that this portal, which was fifty cubits in height, was adorned after a most costly manner. It also had richer and thicker plates of silver and gold upon its doors than the others.

Directly west of the Court of the Women, and

on a level ten feet above it, was the Court of Israel. An ascent of fifteen semicircular steps led up to this platform, the entrance to which was through the great *Nicanor Gate*.

Still farther to the west was the Court of the Priests on a level three feet higher. Beyond this, and on a platform eight feet above it was the Holy House or Temple proper. In its ground plan it was an exact representation of the Tabernacle, but was double its dimensions. In front of it was a grand portal or arch, which seems to have resembled an Egyptian pylon. It extended thirty feet beyond the main building on each side and rose to the height of 100 cubits. Its front was covered with gold, "and over the entrance was spread out a golden vine, with its branches hanging down from a great height, the largeness and fine workmanship of which was a surprising sight" (Antiq. xv, ii, *3*).

Much controversy has arisen over the exact position of the Holy House and the possibilities of every available spot within the limits of the Haram walls have been earnestly discussed and rigorously tested. The determination of the contour of the mountain by sinking shafts down to the rock, all over the area has made it certain, however, that the available space for such a building was originally very limited. Sir Charles Warren, who is probably the best authority on the natural features of the Temple Hill, reached the conclusion, from a careful comparison of the rock levels, that the Dome of the Rock covers the crest of the ridge upon which the Sanctuary of both Temples was built.

"I have to submit," he says, "that where the sides are as one in two or three, when the ground slopes very nearly in the same degree as does the rock of Gibraltar to the west, it seems incredible that the Temple, a building which was so conspicuous, and which was to perform such an important part in the fortifications of the city, should have been placed down in a hole, or even along the sides of the hill, or anywhere else except on the ridge, where there is just enough room for it to have stood, for it is somewhat flattened on the top.

"Supposing the Temple, then, to have been built on the ridge, we must give up all idea of its having stood at the southwest or northwest angles, for there are the beds of the Tyropean and another valley. It could not have stood at the northwest angle, because Josephus tells us that at the north of the Temple was a valley which Pompey in his attack was obliged to fill partially in; and the only valley which exists about there is that which the northern end of the platform of the Dome of the Rock overlooks."

This conclusion harmonizes with the descriptions given in the Mishna, the works of Josephus, and in the scriptures.

"The Temple," says Josephus, "was seated on a strong hill. Originally the level space on its summit scarcely sufficed for the Sanctuary and the altar, the ground about being abrupt and steep; but Solomon, who built the Sanctuary, having completely walled up the eastern side, a colonnade was built upon the embankment; on the other side the Sanctuary remained exposed. In process of time, however, as people were constantly adding to the embankment, the hill became level and broader.

"They also threw down the northern wall, and enclosed as much ground as the circuit of the Temple at large subsequently occupied. After having surrounded the hill from the base with a triple wall, and accomplished a work which surpassed all expectations, they built the upper boundary walls and the lower court of the Temple.

"The lowest part of the latter they built up from a depth of 300 cubits, and in some places more" (Wars v, 5, 1).

"This," says the prophet Ezekiel, "is the law of the House. Upon the top (rosh) of the mountain, the whole limit thereof round about shall be most holy."

Here the phrase "the whole limit round about the top" exactly accords with the description of Josephus, and indicates a definite spot as the centre of the entire structure. If this central spot were the summit of the mountain it is to be found under the swelling dome which covers the Sakhra, and nowhere else within the limits of the Haram area. This is to-day, as it always has been in the past, the top (rosh) of the Holy Mountain: and here, as all the ancient writers af-

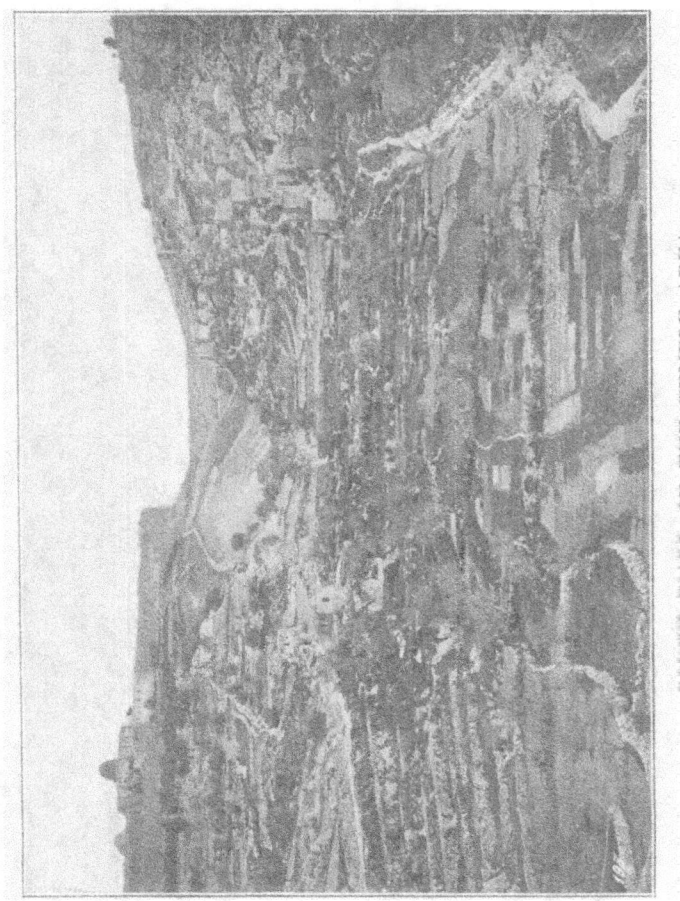

SOUTH WALL OF THE TEMPLE AREA.

The King's Pale and the terraced hillsides which border it are conspicuous features in the foreground.

firm, the first and highest platform was prepared for the Temple and the Altar of Sacrifice.

While this location is generally accepted by modern authorities there still remains a difficulty with respect to the position of the Sakhra within this limit.

Apparently there are only two places where such a mass of bare rock could have been disposed of without marring the symmetry of the Court, or interfering with the ground plan of the buildings which rested upon it.

One was in the Court of the Priests, where it might have been the foundation upon which the Altar of Sacrifice was placed; and the other was in the Holy of Holies, where all of its huge bulk except the summit, or crown, might have been covered by the floor of the Temple.

The advocates of the first position claim that all the conditions and incidental notices which appear in the scriptural account of the selection of the Temple site, are here met and satisfied. This account in its most complete form is given in the 21st chapter of the first book of Chronicles, and may be briefly summarized as follows: —

"And the angel of the Lord stood by the threshing-floor of Ornan (Araunah) the Jebusite. And David lifted up his eyes, and saw the angel of the Lord stand between the earth and the heaven, having a drawn sword in his hand stretched out over Jerusalem. Then David and the elders of Israel, who were clothed in sack-cloth, fell upon their faces. . . . Then the angel of the Lord commanded Gad to say to David, that David should go up, and set up an altar unto the Lord in the threshing-floor of Ornan the Jebusite. And David went up at the saying of Gad, which he spake in the name of the Lord. And Ornan turned back, and saw the angel; and his four sons with him hid themselves. Now Ornan was threshing wheat. And as David came to Ornan, Ornan looked and saw David, and went out of the threshing-floor, and bowed himself to David with his face to the ground." Following this is the account of the purchase of the place of this threshing-floor for which David gave Ornan six hundred shekels of gold by weight. "And David built there an altar unto the Lord, and offered burnt offerings and peace offerings, and called upon the Lord; and He answered him from Heaven by fire upon the altar of burnt offering."

While David was forbidden to build a house for the Lord in this place he gave to his son, Solomon, a solemn charge concerning it. In the subsequent history we are told that Solomon gave heed to this charge and carried out every detail with respect to the place and the plan of the building, as David had instructed him.

"Then Solomon began to build the house of the Lord at Jerusalem in Mount Moriah, where the Lord appeared to David his father, in the place that David had prepared in the threshing-floor of Ornan the Jebusite. And he began to build in the second day of the second month, in the fourth year of his reign."

The minute description of the "place of the Altar" in this narrative seems to accord with all the topographical features of the site which is now covered by the dome of the rock.

On the assumption that the standing place of the angel, "between the earth and the heaven," was the top of the Sakhra every detail concerning the selection of the site, it is alleged, is made clear.

Beside the great stone was the threshing-floor, which would, of necessity, be upon the highest level space, available for such a site, upon the ridge of the mountain. On this platform, or on a small space above it levelled up around the summit of the rock, was the winnowing place for the grain. The hiding-place of Araunah and his sons, from which he came forth as David drew near was the cave at the southeastern end of the rock; and the original purpose of this excavation, with its open mouth at the top, was for the storage of the newly-threshed grain. This would be in accord with the usual custom of the country, where grain is frequently hidden, or stored in dry rock chambers, near the threshing-floors.

On the Sakhra itself there are indications that a framework of some sort has been fitted around it, and this is a confirmation of the supposition that its sides were covered with plates of bronze, and its summit was made, in accordance with Divine direction, the resting-place of the great altar of burnt offering. The elevation of the altar which was reached by a graded ascent from the pavement of the court is regarded as a further confirmation of this supposition. Baedeker, who is usually very cautious in accepting theories which are not supported by positive proofs, says, in his description of the Sakhra, "The probability is that the great sacrificial altar stood here, and traces of a channel for carrying off the blood have been discovered on the rock." To this may be added the testimony of Sir Charles Wilson of the Ordnance Survey, who affirms that "the surface of the rock bears the marks of hard treatment and rough chiselling. On the western side it is cut down to three steps, and on the north side in an irregular shape, the object of which cannot now be discovered." "It is possible also," says Canon Tristram, "that this cave was the receptacle for the offal of the sacrifice and connected with the water supply which was so arranged as to carry off all the refuse of the daily sacrifices without its being seen; this we learn from the rabbinical authorities."

The true value of these conjectures and suggestions can only be determined when permission shall be given to remove the stone which covers the mouth of the mysterious cavity under the rock-cut cave; and also to examine more carefully the contour of the shelving ridge which lies under the floor of the Dome of the Rock. Until then no positive confirmation of the supposition in question can be expected.

The alternative supposition, that the Sakhra occupied a position under the floor of the Temple, except a few inches of its upper surface which rose above the pavement of the Holy of Holies, has a number of able supporters. It is based mainly upon careful measurements and comparisons of rock levels, and also upon certain statements made in the Talmud which give color to the suggestion that the sacred rock of the Moslems is identical with "the Sheteyah," or rock of foundation upon which the Ark of the Covenant was placed. The bearing of these statements upon the question in hand is briefly summed up by Dr. Chaplin as follows:

"On the whole it is difficult to come to any other conclusion than that the stone which the Rabbis write about was a portion of the rock projecting three finger-breadths upward from the floor of the Holy of Holies, covering a cavity which was regarded as the mouth of the abyss, reverenced as the centre and foundation of the world, and having the ineffable name of God inscribed upon it."

It is claimed by some of the advocates of this theory that the Sakhra was a Central Core to the Temple, solid and immovable, "around which all the pavements and courts were built up, and to which they were fastened and united as one solid mass." It is evident, however, that this relation might also exist on the supposition that the position of the Sakhra was in the Court of the Priests; and in this case the Altar, which was located before the House, would be the core around which the mighty structure grew. Indeed it is scarcely possible to conceive of any position which this huge bulk of native rock could occupy except that of a central foundation or core.

The axial line of the temple and its courts seems to have been nearly, if not actually due east, and the "Red Heifer Bridge," which spanned the Kidron Valley, was probably on the same direct line. According to the Mishna the priest who sacrificed the red heifer on the summit of the Mount of Olives could see through or over the eastern gates of the three courts into the place of the Altar, and beyond it to the golden-plated doors in the vestibule of the Holy House itself.

Along this line, in all probability, was the noble ascent, so wonderful in the eyes of the Queen of Sheba, "by which Solomon went up into the house of the Lord."

It was in each of the temples the most notable of all the approaches and naturally became the Via Sacra of the religious processions during the period of the Sacred Festivals.

In one of the earlier visions by the river Chebar the prophet Ezekiel saw the glory of the Lord (the Shekinah) come out from its place in the Temple and pause for a brief space—as though reluctant to depart—over the threshold of the house. From thence, as he beheld, it slowly withdrew and, passing out by the east gate, stood upon the mountain (Olivet) which is on the east side of the city! This departure, as the prophet intimates, was caused by the iniquities and heathen abominations which were tolerated within the precincts of the Sanctuary. In a later vision, when the hearts of the people had turned again to the Lord their God, Ezekiel beheld the reverse of the former vision. Then as he looked the glory of the Lord reappeared and "came into the house by way of the gate, whose prospect was towards the east, and behold the glory of the Lord filled the house."

In the time of our Lord the view of the Temple and its spacious courts from the Mount of Olives must have been singularly beautiful and impressive. Here the whole structure could be seen to best advantage from the lowest range of mosaic pavement and cloistered court to the "place of the Altar," where the smoke of the daily sacrifice ascended in front of the Golden House which crowned the mountain summit. "The Temple," says Josephus, "appeared to strangers, when they were coming to it at a distance, like a mountain covered with snow: for as to those parts of it that were not gilt, they were exceeding white. With respect to its outward face the temple wanted nothing in its front that was likely to surprise either men's minds or their eyes: for it was covered all over with plates of gold of great weight, and, at the first rising of the sun, reflected back a fiery splendor."

Taken as a whole, with its triple walls and embattled towers, and spacious courts, its grand portals and ascents, its galleries and store chambers, its colonnades and cloisters, the Temple was an immense structure, the like of which for beauty and costliness has probably never been equalled on earth. As Milton puts it:

> "The Holy City lifted high her towers
> And higher yet the glorious temple reared
> Her pile far off appearing like a mount
> Of alabaster tipt with golden spires."

Scene follows scene, vision rises upon vision as we attempt to recall the events which have taken place within the limits of this sacred enclosure. In the early dawn of the patriarchal period, when this mountain ridge was an unoccupied site without the walls of Jerusalem, Abraham, and perhaps Melchizedek also, worshipped the Most High God by offering sacrifices upon it. Centuries pass away and, at length, a Jebusite farmer levels a small space upon this breezy height for a threshing floor, and it descends to his posterity, in accordance with the custom of the land, for a possession. By this threshing floor, near the close of David's reign over Israel, the angel of destruction stood in the time of the pestilence with a drawn sword in his hand stretched out over Jerusalem. When in answer to the fervent prayers of David and his people the hand "of the angel that destroyed" was stayed, the deliverance was commemorated by the erection of an altar of sacrifice unto the Lord upon the very spot where the angel sheathed his sword. "Then David said, this is the house of the Lord God, and this is the altar of the burnt offering for Israel" (1 Chron. 22: 1).

From that eventful day until the close of his life David was busied in collecting materials for the house of the Lord, which he purposed in his heart should be "exceeding magnifical of fame and glory throughout all countries." It is estimated that the quantity of gold which he accumulated for this purpose amounted to more than one hundred million dollars: and to this were added a thousand thousand talents of silver. Stone and timber he provided also in abundance, and brass and iron without weight. In the fourth year of the reign of Solomon the foundations of the House of the Lord were laid in the place where the Lord appeared unto David; and with scrupulous fidelity Solomon carried out every detail of the instructions concerning it, which had been communicated to his father by Divine revelation.

For seven years armies of workmen, superintended by the most skillful artisans of Phœnicia and of Israel toiled upon the magnificent structure which grew into beauty and symmetry upon this mountain from day to day and from year to year, without the sound "of hammer or axe or any tool of iron."

When at length all the work was completed, within and without, Solomon assembled the elders of Israel, and the heads of the tribes, the chief of the fathers of the children of Israel unto

Jerusalem to take part in the elaborate dedication ceremonies of the Temple and its courts.

Then—in the language of the sacred historian,—"The priests brought in the ark of the covenant of the Lord unto His place, to the oracle of the house, into the most holy place, even under the wings of the cherubims. . . . And it came to pass, as the trumpeters and singers were as one, to make one sound to be heard in praising and thanking the Lord: and when they lifted up their voice with the trumpets and cymbals and instruments of music, and praised the Lord, saying, 'For He is good; for His mercy endureth forever;' that then the house was filled with a cloud, even the house of the Lord; so that the priests could not stand to minister by reason of the cloud; for the glory of the Lord had filled the house of God" (2 Chron. 5).

"Also, at the same time Solomon kept the feast seven days, and all Israel with him, a very great congregation, from the entering in of Hamath to the River of Egypt. And in the eighth day they made a solemn assembly: for they kept the dedication of the altar seven days, and the feast seven days. And on the three and twentieth day of the seventh month he sent the people away into their tents, glad and merry in heart for the goodness that the Lord had shewed unto David and to Solomon, and to Israel his people."

In the centuries following there have been many joyful assemblages here, in times of special deliverance or at the great festival seasons, but this first dedication festival was, without doubt, the most national in character and in many respects the most notable of all. Its stately rites, its solemn processions, its elaborate ceremonials, its costly sacrifices, its choral and instrumental accompaniments to the sacrificial services, its solemn prayers; and, to crown all, the visible attestation of the Divine presence and favor,— mark this occasion as the most memorable of its kind in the long history of the Church of God.

In contrast with this national revival of religious fervor and loyalty, which seemed to give fair promise of a better day for the world, it is sad to recall the defections, the idolatries, blasphemies, murders and hypocrisies which so soon after dishonored and defiled this holy place. With these came awful denunciations of sin, and judgments more terrible than have ever been inflicted upon any other place or people. Words would be inadequate, and time would fail, to describe the revolutions, rebellions, sieges, famines, desolations, restorations, and wholesale destructions which have here occurred; and the mention of them would include a fragment of the history of almost every nation and race upon the face of the earth.

Within the limits of these time-honored, battle-stained Haram walls two of the costliest buildings ever reared by human hands have flamed heavenward, as beacon-lights of impending doom,—a magnificent holocaust, in each case of cedar and fir; of gold and silver; of marble and precious stones—while hecatombs of human victims filled the outer courts and every foot of pavement and open space around was literally drenched in human blood.

If the hosts that have fallen in deadly conflict in and about the precincts of this holy place could be summed up in order, from the invasion of Shishak, King of Egypt to the recovery of Jerusalem by Saladin, the number would be so large as to seem almost incredible. In the vain, yet desperately heroic attempts that were made to defend it against the successive attacks of the armies of Egypt, Assyria, Babylonia, Macedonia and Syria, unnumbered thousands yielded up their lives. When, after a long and desperate resistance its outer defenses were taken by Pompey, 12,000 of its defenders were put to the sword; when later it fell into the hands of Titus more than 16,000 persons who had fled to it as a last refuge, perished in the flames or by the sword. In that awful hour "the place and nation" of the covenant people "were taken away."

Nearly a thousand years later in the history of the world, when Crusader and Saracen contended, in turn, for the Temple site, the former scenes of horror and destruction were reenacted. The capture of Jerusalem by the Crusaders on the 15th of July, 1099, was followed by a carnival of riot and carnage which lasted nearly a week. With a bigotry as fierce and intolerant as the Jew and hatred as cruel and implacable as the Roman, the followers of Godfrey and Tancred and Raymond pursued the unresisting inhabitants of the city, Moslems and Jews, from refuge to refuge, slaughtering right and left, and sparing neither age nor sex, until scarcely enough of its defenders were left, out of a population estimated at 40,000 to 70,000, to bury the dead. Within the limits of the Haram, where a large number had sought protection, more than 10,000 were put to the sword. Like to this in ferocity, but not so appalling in point of numbers was the massacre, in turn, of all the Christians in Jerusalem—for the most part resident priests and monks—by the Kharezmian hordes in the year 1244. This massacre followed the last of the score, or more, of disastrous sieges, which have heaped ruin upon ruin within and without the walls of the city.

For more than six and a half centuries Jerusalem has been in reality what its name originally implied, a City of Peace: and the place of the "Noble Sanctuary" has been throughout this period, a secluded spot, where flowers bloom, and birds sing and eternal quiet seems to reign. Terrible have been its baptisms of blood, but wonderful beyond all conception have been the far-reaching influences which have gone out from it to bless and elevate mankind. The evil and the good, the unholy and the holy have met here in sharpest contrast, and have ever antagonized each other, but the "fittest has survived" because the Almighty reigns and makes even the wrath of man to accomplish His holy purposes.

"Thus," as one has expressed it, "these massive and time-worn foundations lead us, by a chain of great links, from the current hour to the Father of the Faithful Himself, and the inauguration of God's visible kingdom on earth. These links bind together the whole Bible history; nor can the chain be broken. It is impossible to account for one of the links without admitting the rest of the chain. These weather-beaten stones, therefore, are witnesses, silent, solemn, and unimpeachable, to the great historic facts upon which our faith depends, and on which it has its foundations."

"Standing here," says Dr. Norman Macleod, "one loves to linger on earlier days, and to recall the holy men and women, the kings, priests, and prophets, who came up to this spot to pray—whose faith is our own, whose sayings are our guide, whose life is our example, and whose songs are our hymns of worship. We seem to hear the majestic psalms of David which have ascended from this spot, and have never been silent since on earth, nor will be until they are absorbed into the worship of the Temple above."

All this and much more this Sacred Area suggests to the reverent, thoughtful mind, but what pen can describe, what tongue can tell the full significance, the holy memories, the thronging events, the typical unfoldings, the spirit voices, the unuttered and unutterable longings and aspirations which are, and forever will be, associated with this place. Its material glory has indeed departed but its silent spiritual influence is ruling the world to-day.

Crowned in the olden time with the Sanctuary of Jehovah; illuminated with the brightness of His glory; trodden by the feet of Patriarchs, Prophets, Priests and Kings; and, more than all, hallowed by the presence of the eternal Son of God, "the desire of all nations," who combined in His person and work all that temple and type and priest and sacrifice represented,—this place stands unchallenged among the holy places as the most interesting and memorable on earth.

XII

THE POOL OF SILOAM

ONE of the most interesting monuments of the past in or about Jerusalem is the Pool of Siloam. The name by which it was known in the time of Christ has come down to us unchanged, in the language of the country, and the genuineness of the site has been established beyond question by several converging lines of evidence. It is mentioned by Josephus, Eusebius, Jerome and a host of travellers who have visited Jerusalem in the centuries following. Some of the most notable witnesses in this line of succession are—the Bordeaux Pilgrim (A. D. *333*), Antoninus Martyr (560–570), Arculfus (670), Bernard the Monk (865), Saewulf (1102), Benjamin of Tudela (1163), Fabri (1483), Tsudi (1519), and Maundrell (1697). Nearly all of these travellers since the date of Antoninus make mention of a church which was built over the pool.

The Pool of Siloam is situated in a slight depression on the west side of Ophel—the southern extension of Mount Moriah—near the mouth of the Tyropœan Valley.

The village of Siloam (Silwan), the modern representative of the town mentioned by our Lord, in connection with the fall of its tower,

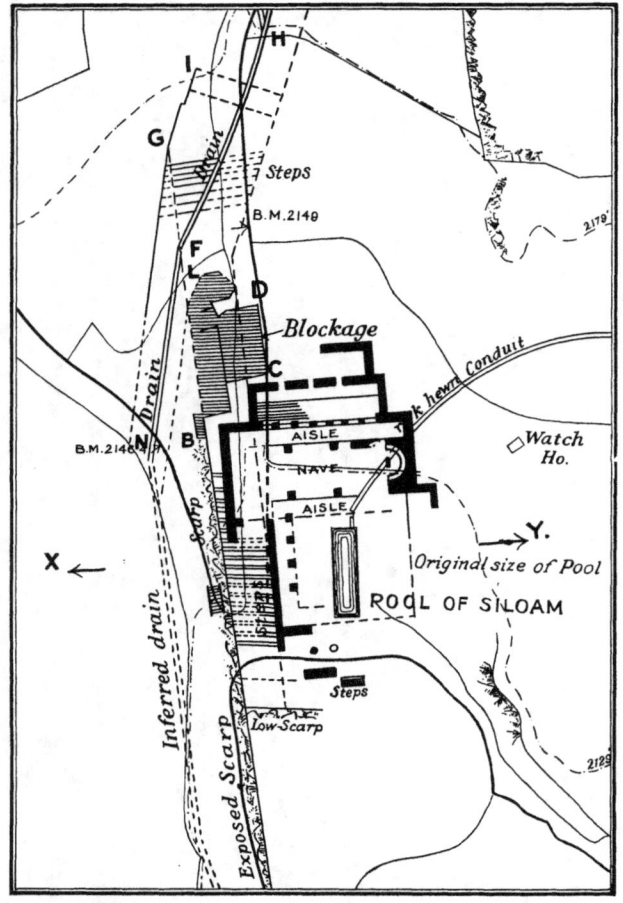

SKETCH PLAN OF RECENT EXCAVATIONS IN
AND ABOUT THE POOL OF SILOAM.
(Reproduced by permission from Report of Dr. Bliss in
Palestine Exploration Quarterly.)

extends along the summit of a low ridge almost directly opposite on the eastern side of the Kidron.

The pool is an artificial receptacle or reservoir, partly hewn out of the rock and partly built up with masonry. It is wholly dependent for its supply of water upon the overflow from the basin of the so-called Fountain of the Virgin on the other side of the ridge of Ophel. This fountain has been identified with En Rogel, the spring of the Fuller, mentioned several times in the Old Testament. The suggestion that it is also identical with the upper pool, or Spring of Gihon ("the spring head"), and that the Pool of Siloam represents the lower Gihon, has met with favor and bids fair to solve some difficulties in connection with the history of these sources of water supply. The visible source of En Rogel is a cave, artificially enlarged, which lies twenty-five feet below the surface of the ground. It is probable that the stream from this source originally ran out at the foot of the hill, and that the excavation was afterwards made at a higher level for the purpose of diverting it in another direction. The bottom of the cave, in which the water rises at irregular intervals, is reached by two flights of stone steps, numbering thirty in all. The connection between this spring, the only fountain of flowing water in or about modern Jerusalem, and the pool of Siloam, is a winding, subterranean conduit, cut through the intervening spur of Ophel, some twenty-six centuries ago. This conduit or tunnel has been explored from end to end by Dr. Robinson, Colonel Warren and others, and its actual measurement in length is seventeen hundred feet. Its height above the floor of the passage varies from a maximum of sixteen feet to a minimum of less than two feet.

While workmen were engaged in making repairs in the basin of the Virgin's Fount they found the entrance to an old rock-hewn aqueduct on the south side, under an accumulation of mud and rock. This aqueduct was traced for nearly 200 feet from its mouth. Its general direction at first was down the valley, but afterwards it seemed to make a great sweep towards the west.

This appears to be the upper part of the tunnel or covered way, which was discovered some years ago by Dr. Schick, and of which he excavated the lower portion for a length of about 600 feet.

It was evidently constructed for the purpose of conveying the water to a reservoir in the lower part of the Tyropœan Valley and is older than the Siloam tunnel.

When Hezekiah "stopped" the spring and made the famous tunnel through the hill of Ophel to the Pool of Siloam the older watercourse was abandoned.

The famous inscription, accidentally discovered near the western mouth of the Siloam tunnel by an Arab boy in 1890, gives the clue to the date as well as the circumstances of its construction. According to this record, which covers the face of a carefully smoothed tablet, twenty-seven inches square,—the excavators began to work simultaneously at both ends of the conduit with the intention of meeting at some point near the middle. They did not meet on a direct line, but when one party had worked a little space beyond the proper meeting-place, the voice of a man belonging to the other part was heard. Guided by the sounds which were then made on either side the workmen were soon " striking pick against pick, one against the other, and the waters flowed from the spring to the pool." It is a notable fact that there are two " *culs de sac* " near the middle of the tunnel, the origin of which can only be explained on the assumption that the excavators worked from different sides towards a meeting point, as indicated in the inscription. The Siloam inscription is justly regarded as one of the most important monumental records of Old Testament times. The characters closely resemble the Phœnician in form, and it is conceded by the leading authorities that this fragment, so long hidden from sight, represents the oldest specimen of the Hebrew language that has come down to us, except the Moabite stone. " This tunnel," says Dr. Ward, " was not made later than the time of King Hezekiah, and the inscription must be of that date or earlier; and it is the only purely Jewish Palestine inscription of any length known, there being nothing else but small seals" (N. Y. *Independent,* '94, p. 553). This discovery certainly confirms, if it does not make certain, the supposition that the conduit and pool were both made by Hezekiah, as recorded in the book of Kings, for the purpose of conducting the water from this outside spring to a convenient spot within the city walls. "The very *raison d'etre* of the Siloam tunnel—as Dr. Bliss puts it —seems to have been to bring water within the limits of the city. It is worthy of note that while we devoted immense labor to testing the contrary theory, yet all our discoveries have tended to support this view." "The Siloam tunnel is ascribed to Hezekiah, says Conder, not solely because in 2 Kings 20: 20, he is said to have made a conduit, but because in 2 Chron. 22: 30, the tunnel is described as leading from Gihon in the *Nakhal,* or Kidron ravine. It has never been proved that there was a second tunnel to Gihon; and the levels of the aqueduct found by Mr. Schick do not agree with such a supposition."

A short distance southeast of the Pool of Siloam is a large reservoir, constructed by building a dam across the valley. It is known as the "Old Pool," and is connected with the upper basin by a broad channel cut in the rock. It seems to have been constructed mainly with a view to conducting the overflow of Siloam to the gardens in the valley below. The waters which glided down this rock-hewn channel, and were parted hither and thither to gladden and refresh the King's Garden at its foot, might well be described as "the waters of Siloah that go softly" (Isa. 9: 6). "It seems probable," says Colonel Wilson, "that the lower pool of Siloam is the mikvah (ditch, R. V. reservoir) which Hezekiah made between the two walls for the water of the old pool (Isa. 22: 11). Thus the construction of the Siloam tunnel, and of the great dam examined by Dr. Bliss would be due to Hezekiah."

Recent excavations (1896–1897) under the direction of the Palestine Exploration Survey Fund have furnished much valuable information with respect to the situation and environment of this sacred pool.

One of the most important results of this work is the discovery that an ancient city wall, clearly distinguishable from a wall of later construction alongside, attributed to the Empress Eudosia, crossed the mouth of the Tyropœan Valley below the Old Pool. In his official report, Dr. Bliss states that this wall, which was buttressed and built without lime, was traced with more or less interruption—but always the same wall—from the Protestant Cemetery on Mount Zion down to a point southwest of the Pool of Siloam, and thence in a northeasterly direction to a point nearly in the centre of the Tyropœan Valley, including within the city of that period the lower as well as the upper pool. There are evidences of frequent reparations along the line of the wall, but it has the same general characteristics throughout and is evidently of a piece with the old wall on Ophel, traced by Warren, which runs towards it from the southeast corner of the Temple area. A gateway, which corresponds in position and surroundings to the Fountain Gate of Scripture, was found in this wall almost directly south of the Siloam pool. Excavations were made at several points north of the pool with the expectation of finding a city wall running across the valley, as indicated apparently by Josephus, but no trace of any wall in this position could be found. At the southwest corner of the Old Pool, however, a wall was found, diverging from the main line, which ran in a northwesterly direction up the west bank of the Tyropean Valley. This was traced to a point some distance beyond the upper pool, and thence all traces of it were lost. The probability is that the material used in its construction had been carried away to rebuild other structures. Dr. Bliss offers the following as a possible explanation of the passages in which Josephus seems to exclude the Pool from the wall he describes:

"First comes the statement in Wars v., 4, 2, where Josephus speaks of the bending of the wall above the Fountain of Siloam. This is taken by some to mean a curve to the north of the pool which it excludes from the city. But our plan—in the April *Quarterly*—shows how, after crossing the Tyropean outside the Old Pool, the wall turns at Ophel, where it overlooks the pool in a way that might well be called 'a bend above Siloam.'

"In regard to the other question, as to whether the Pool was outside the city at the time of Josephus, note that he says 'The *Fountain* of Siloam.' It is quite possible that the term Siloam might be applied equally to the Virgin's Fountain as the source of the waters which fed the Pool of Siloam. That spring was, according to any theory or discovery, outside the city at the time of Josephus, and at every time."

While excavating in the immediate vicinity of the Pool of Siloam the discovery was made that the modern pool—fifty-three feet long by eighteen feet wide—was a contraction within the area of the original basin, which was almost square. As restored it measures seventy-five feet on its north side and seventy-one on the west. Near the northwest corner of the enclosing wall a pier was found at the height of twelve feet nine inches from the pavement with the springer of an arch, which indicated the existence of an arcade at one time on that side of the pool. From this and other indications Dr. Bliss assumes that the arcade ran around the four sides of the pool and represented the "quadriporticum," or four-sided arcade of the Bordeaux Pilgrim.

Directly north of the present pool the remains of an ancient church were found. This building with its appendages was found to be 115 feet in length and 100 feet in breadth. It belongs without doubt to the Byzantine period and was probably built by the Empress Eudosia. The church is mentioned for the first time by Antoninus Martyr (560-570 A. D.). In its present form there are evidences of changes in outline and proportions which indicate one or more restorations. By driving a series of tunnels the general features of the plan were recovered, but the superincumbent mass of earth and débris resting upon the building to the depth of twelve to thirty feet was not removed.

The most interesting discovery, however, in connection with this series of excavations was a grand flight of stone steps on the west side of the old wall leading from the Pool of Siloam up towards the city. The main part of this stairway, as seen by Dr. Bliss, consisted of steps built of hard, well-jointed stones, laid on a bed of chips and mortar. It was evident also that the builders of this stairway had made use of a system of rock-hewn steps of an earlier date. "Though well polished by foot-wear," says Dr. Bliss, "they are very rudely cut, in great contrast to the well-squared stone steps, and the two cannot be ascribed to the same constructors." "On the west the steps butt up against the scarp, and on the east against the west wall of the original pool, which also served as their parapet. As the scarp and wall are not parallel, the breadth of the steps varies from twenty-seven feet at the top to twenty-two feet at the bottom. The number of steps is thirty-four. They vary in height from six to nine and one-half inches, and are arranged in a system of wide and narrow treads alternately, the wide treads from four feet three inches to four feet eleven and one-half inches, and the narrow ones from eleven inches to seventeen."

At some points on the eastern edge of the stairway, it was found that the steps had been broken off to make room for the wall of the church, while at other places they were buried beneath the level of the flooring. These indications furnish indisputable evidence that the stairway was older than the church.

Above the flight of steps a large mass of blockage was found, and beyond this a paved road was traced for a considerable distance. The paved road and the steps were of the same class of work and the general direction pointed towards the entrance in the south wall of the Temple area, known as the Double Gate. A slight divergence to the left would connect it also with the entrance at Robinson's Arch. Dr. Bliss found that the mass of blockage between the steps and the paved road had no connection with any part of the city wall, and hence he concludes that it represents the ruins of some structure which belongs to a period following the disuse of the steps. It is evident, as he expresses it, "that so magnificent a stairway must have had a clear space in front of it."

On the south side of the old wall of the Pool a paved court was uncovered. To this court, or entrance-way, steps led down from an extensive pavement at the foot of the great stairway.

The enlarged basin which Dr. Bliss and his associates have thus recovered, piece by piece, is without doubt the Biblical Pool of Siloam; and it is safe to say that no other site in or near the Holy City has furnished so many interesting mementos of the hoary past. Most of the wall and buildings and other monuments of solid construction to which reference has been made, have been covered up again and are now resting beneath barley fields and cauliflower beds; but the secret of their story and environment has been disclosed and now it is possible to reproduce the prominent features of this sacred site, with its approaches and surroundings as it appeared in the time of Christ.

We can hardly be far wrong in saying, in this connection, that we have along the line of the ancient thoroughfare, extending from the Temple hill to Siloam, and thence to the passageway southward between the walls,—the identical sites of the long lost "Gate of the Fountain," the "wall of the Pool of Siloah by the King's garden," and possibly the very "stairs that go down from the city of David" (Neh. 3: 15).

Down this roadway to Gihon—if we are right in assuming that Gihon was identical with Siloam—a silent procession came more than a thousand years before the time of our Lord, with the three worthies, Zadok, Nathan and Benaiah at their head, to anoint Solomon as King in the room of his father, David. Here, as the holy oil was poured upon his head, the blare of trumpets rang out and reverberated among the rocks, and the shout of the rejoicing multitude arose to the heights above, and was heard by Adonijah and his band of conspirators at En Rogel, on the other side of the ridge of Ophel.

In later times Siloam and the gardens below it became a favorite resort of the pilgrim hosts, which thronged the Holy City at the feasts, and especially at the Feast of Tabernacles—the great harvest festival of the nation—when booths of green branches were erected on the housetops, and in every open space within and about Jerusalem. From Siloam, whose source, like the sacred stream of Ezekiel's vision, was hidden in the very heart of the Temple hill, the water was brought in a golden pitcher at the head of a grand procession, and with great ceremony, for the symbolic libation at the Altar of Sacrifice, on the last great day of the feast. Here, while trumpets sounded and the Temple courts rang with shouts of joy and psalms of praise, the water was poured out by the Priest in commemoration of the waters which flowed out for the thirsty multitude in the wilderness, from the rock of Rephidim. It was doubtless in connection with this service, the most joyous of all the ceremonies of the day, that our Lord stood and cried, saying, "If any man thirst let him come unto Me and drink."

That which makes this place forever memorable and sacred, however, is the story of the healing of the man, blind from his birth, who came hither to wash his clay-covered eyes, in obedience to the command of Jesus. The paved street and the majestic flight of stone steps suggest the route by which the blind man reached the healing waters of the pool. To Siloam, which by its very name was a symbol of Him who was *sent* to be the light of the world, he groped his way with clouded eyes and hesitating step; but in an instant, as he washed the cloudy film came off with the grimy covering of clay; and lo! a new world burst upon his astonished gaze. The first glimpse of this new world centred in the sacred pool and its surroundings. There was a glory on rock and water, on field and hillside and overarching sky, such as he had never even conceived of before, but as he ran up the mountain "like a pleased child," a wider outlook came within the range of vision, and crowning all on the heights above was the Holy City with its gleaming pile of marble and gold. All this and more than words can express, is implied in the brief sentence of the Evangelist: "He came seeing."

XIII

THE WAY TO JERICHO

The historic roadway, which for more than three thousand years has connected Jerusalem with Jericho, is literally a Way of the Wilderness. It enters the wilderness of Judea at the very outskirts of the town of Bethany, and emerges from it on the eastern end of the Jordan plain, hard by the foot of the Tell, which marks the site of the ancient city of Jericho.

The distance between Jerusalem and Jericho, as the road goes, is a little short of seventeen miles. Its general direction is northeast, but it takes advantage, as far as possible, of every available glen, and torrent-bed, and depressed ridge, along the line of its rugged course. There are but few places, therefore, where a change in the road-bed would be practicable; and, as a matter of fact, the broad carriage road, by which tourists now go down to the plain, is merely a widening out, and a filling up of washed out sections of the old historic road. This notable improvement was effected by a force of eight hundred men in the spring of 1889. The rocky ridges, which in the course of the centuries had encroached upon the shrunken bridle path, were cut away, the loose stones were carefully gathered out, and made to serve as a parapet on the danger side of the road, and the rough places, in a comparative sense, at least, were made smooth. It goes without saying that the Roman road between the capital city of Judea and the garden city of the plain, which Herod the Great enlarged and adorned with the costliest and most magnificent buildings, and from which Mark Antony and his successors derived princely revenues, was not a narrow trail or bridal path, such as Dr. Robinson found on his first visit to the Jordan Valley. It must have been a road in keeping with the condition of the great cities which it bound together, and the relation which it necessarily held to the Jordan fords and the rich and prosperous regions beyond. Here, as in every other part of Palestine, the wash and waste of the centuries have effected great changes, and even the highways of ancient times have lost their distinctive features, and have shrunken into camel paths or mountain trails.

The rugged district traversed by this road is the northern portion of the Jeshimon or wilderness, which includes the whole of the eastern slope, or declivity, of the "hill country" of Judea. It is cleft and seamed by numerous torrent beds, which deepen as they descend towards the plain, and these are ofttimes bordered by jagged cliffs or loose irregular masses of bare limestone rock. "Everywhere," as Dr. Robinson puts it, "the slope is steep and sometimes precipitous, and is often cleft to its base by the deep valleys and gorges that issue from the mountain. All is irregular and wild; presenting scenes of savage grandeur." Through all the centuries in which it has been known to history this has been a waste, uncultivated region—save in a few favored spots—a region given over to hermits and wild beasts, to outlaws in hiding, or to wandering shepherds and herdsmen. It was "the land not inhabited," and yet close to the very outskirts of the Holy City, into which the scapegoat was led "by the hand of a fit man," after the iniquities of the people had been confessed and put upon his head.

It is not strange, in view of these characteristic features, that the Jericho road has always been a dangerous way to those who travel it alone. "The very scenery," says Buckingham, "in a portion of the road, the bold projecting crags, the dark shadows in which everything lies buried below the towering heights of the cliffs above, and the forbidding desolation which everywhere reigns around, seem to tempt to robbery and murder, and occasion a dread of it in those who pass that way." The history of the road for many centuries forbids the assumption that this is merely the fancy of a passing traveller. It has long been known as "the Bloody Way," and to this day those who travel over it are safeguarded by representatives of the Turkish government.

It follows from what has been stated, also, that the passageway from Jerusalem to Jericho is a *descent* or "*going down*," of more than ordinary steepness. In a distance of less than fifteen miles, in an air line, the actual descent is nearly thirty-five hundred feet. In other words, it is a letting down from an elevation of more than twenty-five hundred feet to a depression below the sea of nearly nine hundred feet.

Passing from these general statements, we note some points of special interest along the line of this famous route. From Jerusalem to Bethany its course over the southern slope of the Mount of Olives is familiar to every reader of the Bible. The outlook so graphically described by Dean Stanley, from which Jesus beheld the city and wept over it, is at a point where the well-worn roadway passes around a projecting ledge of rock and begins to descend towards Bethany. On the very edge of the little basin in which the town of Mary and Martha lies, the wilderness, and the continuous down-going to the Jordan plain, begin.

At the foot of an incline, which is said to be the steepest in grade along the entire route, the road enters the Wady el Hod, the "valley of the watering place," which it follows for a considerable distance. In this wady there is a famous spring by the roadside,—Ain el Hod,—which has given its name to the valley, and which from time immemorial has been a favorite resting-place for travellers and pilgrims going up to Jerusalem. It is the only fountain of water along the line of this wilderness route, and is supposed to be identical with "the waters of En Shemesh," on the border of Benjamin, to which reference is made in the book of Joshua (15: 7). Tradition has given to it the name of "The Apostle's Fountain." "This name was given it," says Maundrell, "because, as the tradition goes, those holy men were wont to refresh themselves here in their frequent travels between Jerusalem and Jericho. And, indeed, it is a thing very probable, and no more than I believe is done by all that travel this way, the fountain being close by the roadside, and very inviting to the thirsty traveller." The ruins of a large building are scattered about the spring, and an old Saracenic arch covers the stone trough which still receives its refreshing waters. Some three or four miles from the fountain the road leaves the Wady el Hod and crosses a rocky ridge to the Wady es Sidr. Following this for a short distance, it crosses another ridge to the head of the Wady Tal 'at ed Dumm, which it follows almost to the south bank of the Wady Kelt. For the remaining portion of the distance to the plain the road winds around the south side of the wild gorge of the Kelt or Valley of Achor as it was called in the days of Joshua. Near the head of the Wady Tal 'at ed Dumm, and about half way to Jericho, there is a spot of evil omen, where tradition has localized the scene of the parable of the Good Samaritan. A khan has been erected here on the ruins of a similar building of earlier date. This is one of the wildest and most desolate places along the line of the road, and has for ages been a favorite rendezvous for brigands and robber bands. Here, in 1820, a murderous attack was made upon Sir Francis Henneker, who, like the Jewish traveller long centuries ago, was wounded and robbed and left half dead by the roadside. Above the khan there is a conspicuous ridge of red rock which is known as "the hill or ascent of blood" (Tal 'at ed Dumm). The name suggests the site of "Adummim," a landmark on the northern border of the heritage of Judah, and there is every reason to believe that the road leading up to it from the plain, along the bank of the Wady Kelt, is "the going up to Adummim, which is on the south side of the river" (Joshua 15: 7; 18: 17).

This portion of the route is much more rugged and broken, the mountains being higher, the ravines deeper, the peaks sharper, and the slopes more precipitous. The Wady Kelt is the wildest and deepest ravine on the western side of the Jordan. The stream which glides along its rocky bed is shut in by precipitous cliffs rising to the height of five hundred feet; and their smooth faces are literally honeycombed, in some places, with cells and chapels which were occupied by the hermits of the fourth and succeeding centuries.

There is a famous outlook on this portion of the descent at the head of a pass called Akabet ed Deir, where almost the whole of the Jordan plain with its magnificent background of towering mountains may be seen. "This outlook," says Dr. Thomson, "is justly regarded by tourists as the most impressive along the route from Jerusalem to Jericho. But the attempt to reproduce, by the aid of the pencil or the pen, a panorama so vast and varied, can at best be but partially successful. The sites are too many and too distant to group together in one comprehensive picture, and to be brought out with sufficient distinctness to satisfy the eye of any one who gazes upon the impressive reality."

The Jericho road has many associations with the past; and its history, if written in full, would be one of the most interesting volumes in the great and ever-growing library of works which treat of the geography and history of the Holy Land. It was not a military route, like the road which leads down to the valley of Ajalon through the Bethhoron pass, on the other side of the mountains of Judah; but it has been for more than twenty-five centuries the great caravan and pilgrim route to and from the lower fords of the Jordan. Uncounted hosts were wont to come up by this way, from Galilee and all the regions beyond Jordan, to the great feasts at Jerusalem, from the days of the return from the captivity to the year in which Jerusalem was destroyed. And since that time uncounted hosts of Christian pilgrims, from all quarters of the globe, have travelled over the same route. If sometimes these precipitous cliffs and darkly shadowed glens have echoed the cry of distress, there are many more times when they have rung out on the clear air the joyous strains of "Songs of Degrees," taken up by company after company, as they "lifted up their eyes unto the hills" and realized that each stage of the ascent brought them nearer to the gates of the Holy City. This was the way by which David escaped to the farther side of the Jordan when Absalom sought for his life; and by the same route Zedekiah fled from the burning city of Jerusalem, only to be taken a little later on the plain by his relentless pursuers. It was doubtless the way also by which Pompey, Antony, Herod the Great and other noted generals and governors of Rome passed down in state to Jericho, or up to the capital city of Judah on the summit of the mountain. Somewhere along the line of this road, and in all probability at one of the seasons when multitudes were thronging it on their way to Jerusalem, there was heard "the voice of One crying *in the wilderness,*" "Prepare ye the way of the Lord, make His paths straight." Nowhere else could one find such an audience in the wilderness, and from no other point at such a time would the news spread so rapidly, with respect to the man and His message. Then, as He journeyed slowly down to the Sacred River the road was once more alive with human beings, priests, scribes, pharisees, Sadducees, publicans, soldiers and a vast multitude of the common people crowding together to hear His words or to be baptized of Him in Jordan.

There are two events associated with this road,

however, which far transcend the others in importance and which have invested it with undying interest. One is described in the matchless story of the nameless Samaritan who passed this way, and all unconscious of the reward of deathless fame that awaited him, stooped down to minister, with tender touch and compassionate heart, to a fellow-creature in distress. The other is the last journey of our Lord to Jerusalem, the story of which has been so simply and beautifully told by the evangelists. Up these rocky steeps He toiled on foot, with a great company of pilgrims to the Paschal Feast, well knowing that in a brief while after the triumphal procession on the slopes of Olivet, and the shouts of Hosanna to the King that cometh in the name of the Lord, would come the agony, the betrayal, the mocking, and the frenzied outcry of the fickle multitude, clamoring for His death on the cross.

Hallowed by His footsteps on that memorable errand of mercy and love this Via Mala has become the Via Sacra of the Christian tourist and pilgrim. With every returning spring-time multitudes pass over it, as they have done for long centuries in the past, with praiseful hearts and reverent tread. Of this wilderness road, —the type of the rugged but ever ascending pilgrim way from the city of Destruction to the gates of the *Celestial* City,—we may truly say, in the language of the Christian poet:

"This pilgrim path by Thee was trod,
Jesus, my King, by Thee;
Traced by Thy tears, Thy feet, Thy blood,
In love, in death, for me."

XIV

FORDS OF THE JORDAN

There are two notable fords, or crossings, in the upper valley of the Jordan. One is two miles below the outlet of Lake Huleh and the other is about the same distance above the point where the Jordan enters the Lake of Galilee.

The site of the upper ford, which is unquestionably one of the oldest crossings of the river, is marked by a substantial stone bridge of three pointed arches, dating from the fifteenth century or perhaps earlier. Its modern designation is Jisr Benat Ya'cub—"the Bridge of Jacob's Daughters." The name is indicative of some ancient tradition which associates the place with Jacob's journeyings, but its connection with the daughters of the patriarch is not apparent.

Near the bridge on the eastern side are the remains of an ancient khan. It had a fountain of cut stone in the centre of its court, which was supplied by a conduit from the rocky heights above. A solid Roman roadway, paved with large slabs of basalt, has been traced from the bridge to the khan and thence eastward up the slope of the mountain.

From time immemorial this road has been the great caravan route from Egypt and the Mediterranean coasts to Damascus and the East. It was known as the "Via Maris" in the Middle Ages and in the time of Christ one branch of it led up the Jordan Valley and joined the branch from the Esdraelon plain, on the plain of Gennesaret, near Khan Minyeh. It is still a favorite route for caravans and merchantmen, and it is said that in harvest the passage of camels across the bridge never ceases. At this point in all probability Saul of Tarsus "breathing out threatening and slaughter against the disciples of the Lord" crossed the Jordan as he journeyed to Damascus. It is an interesting fact that the river at this fording place is on a level with the Mediterranean Sea.

The lower ford was the ordinary crossing place from Gennesaret to the plain of Batihah. An irregular mound of ruins on the eastern side, known as Et Tell, represents the supposed site of the city of Julias (Bethsaida-Julias). Here the multitudes crossed to the desert place on the other side, where Jesus manifested His compassion—as well as His almighty power—by multiplying the five loaves and the two fishes, to supply their urgent need. This ford was close to the region in which Christ spent the greater part of His public ministry, and was probably on the line of some of His eastward missionary journeys.

South of the Sea of Galilee the survey party found and tabulated about forty crossing places, but most of them are available for passage in midsummer only. The principal fords are the connecting links between ancient highways, which approach the river through wadies, and breaks in the mountains, at different points along the line of its tortuous course. They are as changeless with respect to location as the great thoroughfares which lead to them down the rugged defiles of the mountains. Of the ancient, historic fording places, six at least are worthy of special mention.

(1) The first is just below the exit of the Jordan from the Lake of Galilee. It is the crossing place of the road leading from Tiberias to Gadara and the eastern shore of the lake. Passengers are now ferried over in a boat at this point, but in the days of the Romans the river was spanned by a bridge of ten arches. Most of its massive stone piers, some of which are well preserved, are still standing. The Arabs call this broken bridge Jisr Um el Kanatir. "The ford below it," says Dr. Thomson, "would be excellent, were it not for the fragments of the bridge which strew the bottom. The river is about three hundred feet broad, and it is not more than three feet deep, except in early spring."

(2) Another ancient bridge of stone, called the Jisr el Mejami'a, crosses the river at an old fording place about a mile below the junction of the Yarmuk (Hieromax) with the Jordan. Over this bridge, which is in good condition at the present time, caravans and camel trains, laden with the grain of the Hauran and the merchandise of the east, pass year by year in long procession, as

they have done for centuries in the past. The western terminus of this route, which reaches out eastward to Arabia as well as to Gilead and Bashan, was Acre on the Mediterranean. In later times Haifa, at the foot of Mount Carmel, has become the terminal seaport of this overland route. "Up this Great Road of the East—as we may call it"—says Dr. George A. Smith, "have come through all ages the Midianites, the children of the East. In the Roman period it connected the Asian frontier of the Empire with the capital. Chariots, military troops, companies of officials and merchants, passed by this road, between the Greek cities of Jordan and Ptolemais, the port for Rome." The railroad from Haifa to Damascus, under construction at the present time, follows the same route across Lower Galilee, and passes over the river alongside the bridge, which for so many centuries has marked the site of this ancient fording place. There is good reason to believe that our Lord sometimes made use of this passage across the Jordan, especially when journeying between Capernaum and Jerusalem. It is a well known fact that the eastern or Perean side of the river was the favorite route of the pilgrim bands from Galilee. Here the way was smoother, the grass greener and the water supply from intersecting streams more abundant than on the western side of the Jordan. "These streams," says Canon Tristram, "are perennial, and over them wave many a palm-tree; while on the other side the palm is almost extinct."

(3) In the broad open space at the mouth of the valley of Jezreel there are several fording places. One of this group, about a mile north of the junction of the Jalud with the Jordan, has received more attention than the others in recent years, because of its supposed identity with the place called Bethabara in John's gospel (1 : 28). On the survey map it is designated as "Makhadet Abarah." The word "Abarah" meaning "passage" or "ferry," was recognized by Colonel Conder as radically the equivalent of the name Bethabara, and hence he inferred that the true site of the "House of the Ferry"—Beth-Abara— was to be found at this location, on the eastern side of the river. This inference or conclusion was strengthened by the supposed necessity—as he regarded it—for a location which should be within a day's journey of Cana of Galilee. The identification proposed on these grounds, mainly, has been accepted by several leading authorities, but the location does not seem to accord with other contemporary events, which evidently belong to John's ministry in *Judea*. Aside from the fact that Abarah is a descriptive word and might apply with equal propriety to other fords, there is no warrant for the gratuitous assumption of certain hostile critics that only one day intervened between the departure of Christ from Bethabara and His arrival at Cana in Galilee. "The controlling passage"—as Conder expresses it—in John 2: 1, does not necessarily nor naturally convey this impression. Without doing violence

to the language used, it *may* mean the third day after Jesus took His departure from Bethabara; and in this case there would be sufficient time to go from the upper ford near Jericho to Cana: or it may mean the third day after the arrival of Jesus in Galilee, inasmuch as the fact of His purpose to go thither is mentioned in the preceding verses. The most natural interpretation, however, of the reckoning of the evangelist, connects the date of the marriage at Cana with the last named event in the narrative, namely, the interview of Jesus with Nathaniel. In this case the question of distance is eliminated altogether, for the reason that no direct intimation of the place where this interview occurred is given. If it were in Galilee, at or near Nathaniel's home, as seems most probable, the meaning of the "controlling passage" would be freed from all ambiguity. There would thus be but one day—as Alford suggests—between that event and the marriage in Cana.

It is certain, at least, in view of these possible and legitimate interpretations, that the advocates of a lower ford in Judea are not shut up to the impossibility of the accomplishment of a journey of eighty miles in a single day, as Colonel Conder intimates, if this identification, or one in a similar location, is not accepted.

Another ford of this group is on the direct road from Bethshan to Jabesh Gilead. There are several references to this crossing place in the Old Testament (1 Sam. 11: 8–11; 31: 11, 12; 2

Kings 9: 16–21, etc.), and it was the passage most probably used by our Lord and His disciples when passing from the hill country of Galilee or from the plain of Esdraelon to Jerusalem, by way of Perea.

(4) The Damieh ford, just below the junction of the Jabbok, is the well known crossing of the road from Shechem to Mount Gilead. It seems to have been the place of Jacob's passage over the Jordan, and not improbably of Abraham's also, at an earlier date. It is supposed to be the ford where the Ephraemites, who could not say "Shibboleth," were slain by the men of Gilead (Judges 12: 5, 6). A rude ferry-boat carries passengers over this crossing at the present time, but the remains of a Roman bridge a short distance above it furnish the evidence of a better and safer passage in former times. There is a possibility, but no certain evidence, that Jesus passed this way on one of His journeys to the farther side of Jordan.

(5) The most interesting of all the passages of the Jordan in respect to location and sacred associations, is the Nimrim or Nuwaimeh ford at the mouth of the Wady Shaib. It is nearly opposite Jericho and is on the line of the old Roman road from Jerusalem to Rabbath Ammon and Lower Gilead. It is known as the "upper" ford to distinguish it from another crossing, over against Jericho (Makhadet Hajlah) a short distance below the Pilgrim's bathing place.

The Nimrim ford was close to the broad way

—if not itself a part of it—over which the Israelites passed, by platoons dry shod, on the memorable day when the waters of Jordan stood on a heap far up the Ghor, and rolled away to the sea from all the valley below. By this way, more than five centuries later, Elijah came with his faithful friend and associate, Elisha, from Jericho: and " the river that had drawn back at a nation's feet parted at the stroke of one man, and they too went over dry shod." It is a notable fact that one of the two men who communed with Jesus on the transfiguration mount passed from earth on the top of Mt. Nebo on the farther side of Jordan; and the other from the plain which lies at its foot.

There are other associations, however, with this place of still greater interest. On the edge of Wady Shaib, a short distance east of the ford, there is a ruined site, alongside a copious fountain of water, which is known as Beit Nimrim. Its identity with Beth-Nimrah (the house of the leopard) is not questioned. In the Septuagint the word Bethabra (the house of the ford) is substituted for Beth-Nimrah. In this substitution of a different name for the same place we have the only definite clue to the location of Bethabara; and this accords with the indirect testimony of the evangelists which conveys the impression that all the events connected with the baptism of Jesus, and also with the Baptist's testimony concerning Him—presumably given after the Temptation (John 1: 15-37),—took place in the same region. This is spoken of as the place "where John *at first* baptized" (John 10: 40). Then went out to him Jerusalem, and all Judea, and all the region round about Jordan and were baptized of him in Jordan confessing their sins (Matt. 3: 5, 6). At a later date the Baptist was found at Ænon, near Salim, but this was some months after Jesus had entered upon His public ministry.

There is no intimation in the gospel narratives that John had changed his preaching place during the forty days that Jesus was in the wilderness. He was then in the height of his fame; and it seems almost incredible that he should have gone at that time so far north as the supposed site of Bethabara on the eastern border of Galilee: or that a deputation of priests and Levites should have been sent to that place from Jerusalem.

In some of the oldest manuscripts Bethany is found instead of Bethabara, but it is also true that Origen knowing this selected Bethabara as the better or more familiar name. The meaning of the name, as Bloomfield suggests, is almost exactly the same with that of Bethany. "The difficulty may be removed," he says, "by supposing that Bethabara was the original name of the place, but that in the time of Christ it was usually called Bethania, as better designating its situation—the original crossing being by ford, having been changed to that by ferry. In Origen's time the old name may still have been in use and this may have occasioned the change in the reading."

In a word, therefore, all the circumstances of the gospel narratives, as well as the name which the Septuagint supplies, point to this spot beyond Jordan as the place of the baptism of our Lord and of the events following the inquiries of the priests and Levites who were sent to John from Jerusalem. "There is surely a deep significance in the fact," says Dr. Tristram, "if this be so, of him who came in the spirit and power of Elias, thus exercising his function of herald of the kingdom, and completing his mission by the baptism of Christ, at the very spot where his prototype had ceased from his mission and been carried unto heaven. As suddenly as the first Elijah disappeared, so suddenly did the second Elias appear to prepare the way of the Redeemer. Where the first dropped his mantle, in that very spot did the second take it up."

The Nimrim ford was the usual crossing place for those who came up to Jerusalem to the feasts, from Galilee and Perea and here on several occasions Jesus passed over with the multitudes, or in company with His disciples. Here also He abode two days after He had received the message that Lazarus was sick (John 10: 40; 11: 6). A new toll bridge has recently been thrown over the Jordan at the Nimrim ford.

(6) The lower ford, five or six miles below the Nimrim ford, is the traditional site of the baptism of Christ, but there is no evidence except

THE JORDAN BRIDGE AT MOUTH OF WADY SHAIR (NIMRIM FORD).

the tradition itself, in support of this location. It was one of the "fords towards Moab" and the probable crossing place of Naomi and Ruth on their journey to Bethlehem.

XV

THE LAND BEYOND JORDAN

During the period covered by the Old Testament Scriptures the country beyond Jordan, south of the Yarmuk or Hieromax River, was commonly designated as Gilead, or Mount Gilead. When Syria came under the supremacy of Rome, this district was made a separate province, and to it was given the official title of Perea, "the land beyond." In the time of Christ the provinces of Galilee and Perea were united under the rule of Herod Antipas. There are some discrepancies of statement among the writers of that day with respect to the exact limits of Perea. In its narrower sense, as sometimes used, the term Perea included the district now known as the Belka, extending from the Jabbok River to the Arnon. There can be no doubt, however, that the name, in its larger sense, was used to include important places in the immediate vicinity of the Yarmuk River, as well as in the northern portion of the land of Moab.

There are good reasons, therefore, for the generally accepted belief that Perea included, at this time, all the region east of the Jordan to the desert, from the Yarmuk to the Arnon; or, in other words, all of the land of Gilead and the northern portion of the land of Moab.

This district as a whole is noted for the diversity of its physical features, and its extraordinary variety of soil and climate. Its plain is a broad, generous strip of alluvial soil, watered by numerous streams, and teeming with all the products of a tropical land; its hillsides are a succession of rugged slopes and terraces, seamed with water courses and dotted here and there with patches of woodland and pasture-land; its summit is a broad ridge of uneven table-land, celebrated for its picturesque beauty, its luxuriant herbage, its far-famed cattle ranges and its noble forests. At one point in the northern portion of this district there yet remains a grove of two hundred palm-trees of unusual size and beauty; at another, to the south, several clumps of acacia or "shittim" trees. On the slopes above are numerous representatives of the shrubs and trees of hardier growth, and on the summit there are dark groves of oak and Scotch fir. Here, as one has expressed it, "the difference in elevation does not really convey an adequate notion of the difference in climate, owing to the peculiar conditions of the Jordan Valley, which, being depressed below the level of the sea, produces a contrast in vegetation with the mountains of Gilead corresponding rather to a difference of ten thousand feet than of only half that elevation. The consequence is, that in no part of the world could so great a variety of agricultural produce be obtained, compressed within so limited a space." "In all Gilead," says Canon Tristram, "whether forests, prairie, or valley, there is a wild grandeur, unequalled in any other part of Palestine. Lovely knolls and dells open out at every turn, gently rising to the wooded plateau above. Then we rise to the higher ground and ride through noble forests of oak. Then for a mile or more through luxuriant green corn, or perhaps through a rich forest of scattered olive-trees, left untended and uncared for, with perhaps patches of corn in the open glades. No one can fairly judge of Israel's heritage who has not seen the luxuriant exuberage of Gilead, as well as the hard rocks of Judea, which only yield their abundance to reward constant toil and care. To compare the two is to contrast nakedness and luxuriance. Yet the present state of Gilead is just what Western Palestine was in the days of Abraham."

This description, by one who has thoroughly studied the physical features and natural products of every portion of the land, accords with the uniform testimony of all travellers and explorers who have traversed this favored region. In the time of Christ it was not given over to wandering Bedouin and herdsmen, as in our day, but it was the home of a busy, prosperous and energetic people, who built great cities, constructed costly conduits and reservoirs, planted vineyards and olive yards, and skillfully developed the resources of the country. The ruins of several Græco-Roman cities covering acres of ground are the astonishment of modern travellers, and furnish evidence not only of a large population, but of a highly advanced state of civilization and refinement.

The famous cities of the Decapolis, an interleagued group with their outlying towns, were all east of the Jordan, except Bethshan: and six out of the ten were within the limits of the province of Perea. One of this group, now known as Jerash, has been described as probably the most perfect Roman city left above ground. Within its massive walls are temples, theatres, baths, gateways, a forum and clustered columns, more than two hundred of which are yet standing. At Gadara, for a time the capital of Perea, the ruins are over two miles in circuit, and the rich ornamental work in marble, basalt, and granite, lying in confused heaps or scattered everywhere over the ground, indicate the existence of a city of great wealth and magnificence.

It is a noteworthy fact in this connection, that in the beginning of our Lord's public ministry multitudes from "beyond Jordan" and the "Decapolis" followed Him, "as He went about all Galilee," teaching in the synagogues, healing the sick and preaching the gospel of the kingdom (Matt. 4: 23–25).

The trans-Jordanic cities reached the culmination of their material greatness during the age of the Antonines, but there is abundant evidence also with respect to their prosperity, populousness, and dominating influence at the beginning of the Christian Era.

The Jordan has always been a rapid, swirling river, and in Old Testament times it was regarded as a formidable barrier between the eastern and western divisions of the land. At some seasons of the year it is dangerous to attempt the crossing by the fords at any point; and at other times the footing, except in a few places, is treacherous and uncertain. It was not in accordance with the policy of Rome to permit such a barrier to exist between provinces under her rule, and hence in the time of Christ there were substantial bridges of stone at every important crossing between the Sea of Galilee and the mouth of the river. The ruins of several of these bridges yet remain. A network of paved roads, connecting with these crossings, linked all the important towns of Perea together, and gave ready access to the desert khans and fortresses on the frontier line of defense. On this side of the Jordan more than five hundred miles of solid Roman roads have been traced. Over these royal roadways, prepared unwittingly by an alien nation for His coming and for the spread of His gospel, the Redeemer travelled on His journeys to and from Jerusalem, and on His missionary circuit through Galilee, the Decapolis and Perea. "It was up and down these roads," also, as Dr. Geo. Adams Smith has happily put it —"roads which were in touch with Rome and with Babylon—that the immortal figures of the

Parables passed. By them came the merchantmen seeking goodly pearls, the king departing to receive his kingdom, the friend on a journey, the householder arriving suddenly upon his servants, and the prodigal coming back from the far country."

It is a common, but an erroneous impression, that Perea was a semi-heathen district. From all the information attainable, its population was about as distinctively Jewish as the population of Galilee, the province associated with it under the rule of Herod Antipas. The thronging crowds which followed Jesus from Perea in the beginning of His ministry, and the fact that He spent months among similar crowds as He journeyed slowly through this portion of the land near the close of His public ministry, would indicate the existence of a population the mass of which, at least, belonged to the house of Israel. "North of the Yarmuk," says Dr. Smith, "the inhabitants were mainly Greek, and across the Jordan, Samaria was Samaritan; but in Perea, as in Galilee, Jews formed the bulk of the population; and narrow as the strip must have been which connected the two provinces, it formed an easy and convenient passage. The Jews always regarded Perea, Galilee and Judea as the three Jewish provinces; and when the Galilean pilgrims came to the feasts at Jerusalem by Perea, they felt they had travelled all the way on Jewish soil." It was for this reason mainly, it may be added, that the Jews from the north preferred the eastern side of Jordan. On one occasion our Lord made choice of the hill-country road through Samaria in passing from Judea to Galilee, but at other times He seems to have followed the usual route, between these provinces, by way of Perea. The tradition which locates one stage of the return journey of Joseph and Mary at Beeroth, a few miles north of Jerusalem, when Jesus was a child of twelve years, is at best only a conjecture. At this time, as the narrative intimates, they were travelling with a large company of Galileans; and it is extremely improbable that such a party should have chosen the route through Samaria.

The most convenient crossings at that time for those who came from the vicinity of the Lake of Galilee were the bridge just below the outgo of the Jordan from the Lake, or the bridge, called Jisr el Mejami'a, a short distance below the junction of the Yarmuk with the Jordan. Those who came by way of the Esdraelon plain crossed at one of the passages in the vicinity of Bethshan. The well beaten pilgrim route from these passages continued down the valley to the rich plain at the mouth of the Jabbok, and thence to the upper ford of Jericho at the mouth of the Wady Shaib. At this point the river was recrossed and the ascent to the Holy City, by way of Jericho, began.

The land beyond Jordan, in common with the sacred river itself, "blends the memories of the Old and New Covenants." In the early dawn of human history its northern section was traversed by Abraham and Israel. A few centuries later the breezy heights of Gilead were the camping place of the armies of Israel; and thence, after all the land had been subdued, the remove was made to the final encampment on the plains of Moab or Shittim. Here Moses gave to the people a summary or repetition of the Law, as given on Mount Sinai; rehearsed the principal events of their history through the forty years of the wilderness wandering; and, as the representative of Jehovah, closed his long administration of Israel's government with a solemn charge. On the mountain of Pisgah which overshadows this plain, the undimmed eye of Moses beheld the "good land" on the other side of Jordan; and ere the vision had faded away, his freed spirit was summoned into the presence of the Eternal God, with whom, even while on earth, he had ofttimes communed face to face as a man with his friend. Not far from this spot some centuries later two of the noted prophets of Israel, Elijah and Elisha, were holding sweet converse as they journeyed together. Suddenly, as they went on and talked, there was a flash of celestial brightness for a brief moment on the slope of Gilead; and an appearance as it were of a chariot of fire and horses of fire. As the glowing vision swept by, Elijah was separated from his friend and caught up by a whirlwind into the opening heaven. Not without significance, in view of these events, in Old Testament history, was the coming of another prophet in the spirit and power of Elijah, who prepared the way for the long promised Deliverer of Israel, and on this side of Jordan witnessed for Him, not only in words as he stood by the riverside, but also by a martyr's death in a dungeon keep on the heights of Moab. There was a fitting and still more significant blending of the Old and the New, however, when Jesus of Nazareth came into this Perean land from Galilee, and received baptism at the prophet's hands. Then again were the heavens opened and the Spirit of God descended like a dove and rested upon Him; "and lo a voice from heaven, saying, This is My beloved Son, in whom I am well pleased." In Him at this eventful hour were verified all the promises concerning the Prophet like unto Moses; the great High Priest, who should offer atonement for sin; the King who should rule in righteousness; the Shepherd who should lead His people like a flock; and the Lamb of God who should take away the sin of the world.

In the region beyond Jordan Jesus began His itinerant ministry—winning on this ground His first disciples—and here also He ended it. When He took His final departure from the place "where John at first baptized," it was to go up by the most direct route to Jerusalem, where, as He well knew, the cross awaited Him.

To this people in the land beyond Jordan, who gave Him a refuge and a welcome when the Samaritans had refused Him entrance to their villages—when the Galileans had rejected Him and the rulers in Judea were seeking for His life—Jesus gave the most precious things of His beneficent ministry. In Perea He reaped where John had sown, and, as in Galilee, a round of cities and villages was visited. Here He brought joy and gladness to many a desolate heart and afflicted home, although moving Himself under the very shadow of the cross. To this place and period belong the Parables of the Great Supper, the Rich Man and Lazarus, the Pharisee and the Publican, the Lost Sheep, the Prodigal Son and others of like import—comprising about one-third of all the recorded parables of Jesus—which so forcibly and beautifully illustrate the riches of redeeming grace and the wonders of redeeming love. Here, as we read in Luke's gospel—and no marvel that it was so—"all the publicans and sinners *drew near* unto Him" to hear Him: and many from the ranks of the lowly and despised classes of society received His testimony and believed on His name. In Galilee Jesus spoke mainly of the coming *kingdom*, its nature and laws, and the necessity of seeking it above all other things; but here He speaks of the King's Son who was coming to His own, albeit through suffering and shame, and dwelt especially upon the consummation of the long promised blessings of Messiah's reign.

It was in Perea also that the interview with the rich young ruler, and—ever memorable incident—the blessing of the little children, brought to Him by their parents, took place.

In view of this tender and blessed ministry, we do not wonder that Christianity took deep root in the trans-Jordanic provinces after the ascension of our Lord; and that here many were found to be faithful even unto death, through the dark days of persecution in the generations following.

XVI

THE STRONGHOLDS OF MACHÆRUS AND MASADA

THE most interesting remains on the shores of the Dead Sea are the ruined heaps and shattered walls which mark the sites of the ancient fortresses of Machærus and Masada.

The one overlooked the waters of this silent sea from a rugged crest on the heights of Moab: the other from the summit of an isolated crag on the western side, amid the wildest and most desolate portion of the Wilderness of Judea. Both were built in troublous times as places of refuge and defense, both were strongly fortified in the time of our Lord and both have been associated with some of the darkest and most tragic events in human history.

Machærus.—The Castle or Citadel of Machærus was built originally by Alexander Janneus as a bulwark against invasion from the east and south, in the beginning of the century which preceded the birth of Christ. When Aristobulus was hard pressed by the Roman General Gabinius he fled to this stronghold with 1,000 men. He was closely followed, however, by Gabinius, who carried the citadel by assault and afterwards destroyed it. The unusual advantages of the place as a frontier fortress and as a place of refuge in time of danger, were noted by Herod the Great, soon after his accession to power, and under his direction Machærus was rebuilt on a larger scale and fortified with massive walls and towers. At the other end of the narrow ridge on which the citadel was erected Herod built a grand palace of costly material and workmanship, surrounding it with a great wall, the towers of which are said to have been 200 feet high at the corners. Within the enclosure of this palace-fortress were marble-lined halls, magnificent baths, reservoirs, barracks, storehouses and everything which this luxurious ruler regarded as essential to his comfort or security. The detached citadel occupied the most defensible position and was intended to be a last resort in case the palace should be taken.

The location of Machærus is at the northern extremity of Jebel Attarus, one of the highest ridges of the Moabite range. It is seven miles from the Dead Sea and is about 3,800 feet above its surface. From this outlook may be seen, in distinct outline, the whole of the western shore of the Sea, the Wilderness of Judea and the mountains of Judea from Hebron to the higher elevations north of Jerusalem. It is said that the beacon lights on the Mount of Olives, which announced the appearance of the Passover moon, could be seen from Tabor and Machærus.

The narrow ridge on which the citadel was built is almost surrounded by deep valleys with precipitous sides. From this point the ground falls away abruptly northward towards the deep trench-like chasm of the Wady Zerka Ma'in. This is the Callirhoe of ancient times, and next to the cleft through which the Arnon finds its way to the Salt Sea it is the deepest furrow on the western face of the mountains of Moab. At one point it is bordered by cliffs 1,700 feet in height. On the south side basaltic columns rise several hundred feet above the bed of the stream and almost block the entrance to the gorge. Farther down the hot springs, which have made this place a famous resort since the days of the Roman occupation, burst out from the side of the valley, and send up clouds of vapor to the skies. These springs, which vary in temperature from 110 degrees to 140 degrees, are the sources of eight or ten rivulets, some of which glide along between banks of basaltic or limestone rock to the swift stream which courses through the bed of the valley, while others fall in cascades amid luxurious masses of tropical vegetation.

In a vivid description of this weird and awe-inspiring retreat, Colonel Conder says :—"It took a full hour to reach the bottom of the gorge, and the scene beneath was wonderful beyond description. On the south, black basalt, brown limestone, gleaming marl. On the north sandstone cliffs of all colors, from pale yellow to pink purple. In the valley itself the brilliant green of palm clumps, rejoicing in the heat and in the sandy soil. The streams, bursting from the cliffs, poured down in rivulets between banks of crusted orange sulphur deposits. . . . Crossing three rivulets, from each of which our horses, apparently aware of the heat of the water, shrank back in fear, we reached the principal hot spring, which has formed a ledge of breccia-like deposit in the valley, just north of the basalt cliff. Here the chasm is narrowest, and the main stream below could be seen winding among black boulders, which impede its course, with the dark precipice frowning as though about to fall, like Sinai in the Pilgrim's Progress. The stream has bored through the sulphurous breccia, and runs in a tunnel of its own making, issuing from this hot shaft about 100 feet lower, in the gorge itself. . . . Of all scenes in Syria, even after standing on Hermon, or among the groves of Banias, or at Engedi, or among the crags of the Antilebanon, there is none which so dwells in my memory as does this awful gorge, 'the valley of God,' by Beth Peor, where perhaps the body of Moses was laid—the fair flowing stream which Herod sought below the gloomy prison of John the Baptist at Machærus—the dread chasm where the Bedawin still offer sacrifices to the desert spirits, and still bathe with full faith in the healing powers of the spring."

After the death of Herod the Great the provinces of Galilee and Perea were assigned to Herod Antipas; and for more than thirty years the stronghold which overlooked this mysterious valley of the healing waters was in his keeping.

This breezy height was his favorite mountain resort and during his period of rule the palace of

Machærus was the scene of many a brilliant assemblage and dissolute revel. When John the Baptist came out from his retirement in the Wilderness and began to preach and baptize on the Perean side of the Jordan he was in the territory of Herod, and the influence which he exerted was felt in the palace of Machærus as well as in the temple at Jerusalem. Drawn at first by curiosity Herod was impressed by the sincerity and uncompromising fidelity of this famous preacher of righteousness, and while he feared him, as Ahab feared Elijah, he was nevertheless attracted to him, and for a time his better nature assented to the truths which he so earnestly advocated and so strenuously enjoined, without respect to the claims of rank or place or person. It is implied in the narrative of the evangelists—strange as it may seem—that this cruel, crafty and sensual despot had relations with John the Baptist, at this time, based on profound respect, which bordered upon intimacy, if not affection. As Mark puts it: "Herod feared John, knowing that he was a just man and an holy, and *observed* him; and when he heard him he *did many things*, and heard him *gladly*."

The change of attitude towards this faithful prophet was due to the evil influences of Herodias. At her instigation he was seized and cast into prison but she could not at this time, or by the use of direct influences, prevail upon Herod to put him to death. This is plainly intimated in the narrative of the evangelist already quoted:

"For Herod himself had sent forth and laid hold upon John, and bound him in prison *for Herodias' sake,* his brother Philip's wife. For John had said unto Herod, It is not lawful for thee to have thy brother's wife. *Therefore Herodias had a quarrel* against him, and would have killed him, *but she could not*" (Mark 6: 17-19). From the Jewish historian, Josephus, we get the information that the place of John's imprisonment was the castle of Machærus. In one of the dungeon keeps of this gloomy fortress the last and greatest of the Old Testament prophets languished for weary months, before the messenger of death brought to his unfettered spirit the long looked for deliverance. The details of this sad and shameful tragedy are familiar to all. No darker story of revengeful scheming and heartless cruelty sullies the pages of human history; and no braver witness for the truth of God ever sealed the testimony which his lips had uttered with his own heart's blood.

To Herodias, in that brief moment of fancied triumph, was given the gory head of the murdered prophet, but the mangled body, which had probably been cast outside the ramparts, was tenderly taken up by the disciples and reverently prepared for burial. Then, when all was over, "the disciples went and told Jesus."

In the very prime of life the voice of this herald messenger was rudely silenced in death, but not until his message had been delivered and his great life-work accomplished:

"And as flashed the headsman's broadsword: rose the Sun on
   Pisgah's height
And the Morning Star was hidden in the flash of golden
   light."

Among the ruins of Machærus two underground, rock-hewn chambers have been found which in all probability were the lower vaults of the prison house in which John the Baptist was confined. Dr. Tristram, the first European explorer who visited and described the place, examined these chambers or cells with care. One was partly destroyed, but the other was very deep and its sides were scarcely broken in. "That these were dungeons," he says, "not cisterns, is evident from there being no traces of cement, which never perishes from the walls of ancient reservoirs, and from the small holes, still visible in the masonry, where staples of wood and iron had once been fixed. One of these must surely have been the prison house of John the Baptist."

About forty years later Machærus was the scene of another dark tragedy in connection with the last great war of the Jews with Rome. During this long period of strife, or near its close, the three strongholds of Southern Palestine,—Machærus, Herodium, and Masada,—were occupied and held by insurgent bands of the Zealots or Sicarii, who exacted tribute from the defenseless communities around them, and, with reckless courage, defied the veteran legions, which, after the fall of Jerusalem, were sent to subdue them.

After the Procurator, Lucilius Bassus, had taken the Citadel of the Herodium, he collected all the available soldiers of the province, and crossing the Jordan laid siege to the fortress of Machærus.

During the progress of the siege several sorties were made by the garrison, and in one of these ventures Eleazer, a noted leader of the Jews, was taken prisoner.

Through his intercession, when threatened with instant death by crucifixion, the Citadel was surrendered to the Romans. The parties directly concerned in this surrender were spared but the rest of the garrison, while attempting to escape, were pursued by the soldiers and put to the sword. According to Josephus, one thousand and seven hundred of the defenders of the garrison were slain, while all the women and children were sold into slavery.

When the sun arose over the heights of Moab, on the morning which followed that day of ruthless slaughter, it shone upon dismantled walls and desolate heaps of rocks, covered with dead bodies and crimsoned with human blood.

Masada.—After the fall of Machærus this gloomy fortress of the wilderness was the only remaining stronghold of the insurgents, within the limits of the Holy Land. Here in the very heart of the most desolate region of Judea the last stand was made against Rome. In this fateful spot where the last vial of wrath was poured out, amid smoke and flame, the clash of arms, and the

PORTION OF WALL AND GATEWAY ON NORTHERN EDGE OF SUMMIT OF THE HILL OF MASADA.

groans of self-immolated victims, the doom of the Jewish nation was sealed.

The site of Masada, now known as Sebbeh, has been identified with certainty by the remains of the Roman wall of circumvallation as well as by the massive walls, partially preserved in places, which surrounded the fortress itself.

The isolated hill or crag upon which Masada was built is one of the highest and most precipitous of the towering cliffs of the great mountain wall, which border the western shore of the Dead Sea. It is about twelve miles south of Engedi, and the easiest way of approach to it from the highlands of Judea is by way of the pass which leads down to the coast at this point. Dr. George A. Smith found traces of a "military" road, designed originally for wheeled vehicles, between Engedi and Masada, but at the present time the narrow bridle-path into which it has shrunken, is scarcely passable, in many places, for travellers on horseback. In its higher levels near the ruined fortress the track of this ancient roadway has wholly disappeared.

The supposition advanced by Dr. Smith that this was an "inland passageway, connecting the fortresses of Masada and Herodium" is doubtless correct. Masada may be approached, also, from Jebel Usdum to the south and from Hebron by a rugged mountain trail, involving a journey of ten or twelve hours.

It has been said with truth that the fortresses are very few that match Masada in natural strength. Its site was a refuge for wild goats before it became a refuge for hunted men, and in its best estate it was a desert hold, remote from civilization and from all the ordinary routes of travel. At the foot of the storm shattered cliff upon which it rested was the Dead Sea, occupying the deepest basin on the land surface of the earth; behind it was a rugged background of jagged rock and deeply furrowed desert waste, reaching up by precipitous ascents and terraced slopes to the plateau, or hill country of Judea, more than twenty five hundred feet above it, while on every side "vastly deep chasms," as Josephus terms them, cut it off from the towering cliffs around it.

On the seaward side the citadel was seventeen hundred feet above the water level. On the north and south sides the cliff rose to the height of thirteen or fourteen hundred feet. On the west side there is a partial connection with the main ridge from the summit of a slope or undercliff, about one thousand feet high, which at this point abuts against the fortified hill. This is the one vulnerable point in the entire circuit, and yet it lies about four hundred feet below the top of the great rock. From this ledge a narrow, zigzag pathway, hewn out of the rock and guarded at every exposed point, ascended to the gate of the castle. Josephus describes another approach from the eastern side, "which was called the serpent, as resembling that animal in its narrowness and its perpetual windings."

Colonel Warren of the survey party ascended this pathway to the summit, but it was a difficult and dangerous venture.

The summit of the great rock is an oblong, almost level plateau. Its length from north to south is about two thousand feet, and its breadth from six hundred to eight hundred feet, the widest part being at the southern extremity.

The outlook from this elevated platform includes the long wall of the mountains of Moab, the whole of the Dead Sea, the coast plain on its western side from Engedi to Jebel Usdum, and a limited view, to which reference has been already made, of the desolate wastes of the Judean wilderness.

Upon this great rock, so strangely uplifted amid the desert solitudes, Jonathan Maccabeus built a castle, about the middle of the second century before Christ and called it Masada,—the stronghold. In the time of Hyrcanus II it was regarded as the strongest of all the fortified places of Judea, and when Antigonus invaded Judea and besieged Jerusalem Herod fled to Masada with his bride, Mariamne, for safety. At a later period Herod built a massive wall around the entire summit and strengthened it with thirty-eight towers. Within the ramparts he enlarged and strengthened the citadel and added several buildings of lesser dimensions for barracks and storehouses. On the western side he also erected a stately palace, adorned with costly marbles and mosaics, and lavishly provided with every comfort and luxury. An abundant supply of water for the use of the garrison, and for times of emergency, was secured during the seasons of rain, and stored in capacious reservoirs hewn out of the rock. In the centre of the plateau a large space was also reserved for cultivation. The soil within this reservation was said to be very rich, and the greatest portion of it was probably carried up from the adjacent valleys. In view of the possibility of a protracted siege immense stores of grain, oil, pulse wine and dates were laid up in caverns and hidden chambers among the rocks, and in the citadel there were arms and equipments for ten thousand men. These elaborate preparations "show," says the Jewish historian, "that Herod had taken much pains to have all things ready for the greatest occasions; for the report goes how he thus prepared this fortress on his own account, as a refuge against two kinds of danger; the one of fear of the multitude of the Jews, lest they should depose him, and restore their former kings to the government; the other danger was greater and more terrible, which arose from Cleopatra, queen of Egypt, who did not conceal her intentions, but spoke often to Antony, and desired him to cut off Herod, and entreated him to bestow the kingdom of Judea upon her."

The time never came in Herod's day when this provision for an evil hour was needed, but when all of the Herodian line had passed away it fell into the hands of a band of desperate men, who, like this crafty and cruel king, were pursued by an avenging angel; and whose awful end closes one of the saddest and most tragic chapters in the annals of ancient history.

The possessors of this fateful inheritance were an independent clan of the fanatical Sicarii, under the leadership of Eleazer, a descendant of Judas of Galilee. At the very beginning of the war with Vespasian, Eleazer captured Masada by stratagem and held it, without opposition on the part of the Romans, until Jerusalem, and all the other strongholds in Judea, had fallen into their hands.

Availing themselves of the immense stores of arms and provisions which Herod had laid up, and which Josephus assures us were still in good condition, Eleazer and his men strengthened the fortress at all the exposed points and encouraged each other in the high resolve to hold it against all odds, or failing in this to perish within its walls.

It fell to the lot of Flavius Silva, the Procurator who succeeded Lucilius Bassus, to attempt the reduction of this formidable stronghold. Collecting an army from every part of the country Silva made careful and deliberate preparation, beforehand, to meet all the contingencies which might arise in connection with this difficult and perilous undertaking. There is scarcely an example in history where so many obstacles of an unusual character had to be met and overcome, or where the dauntless energy, the engineering skill and the dogged persistency of the Roman soldier of that age, were more strikingly displayed.

While the garrison had a sufficient supply of food and water, and also of arms and material for defense, it was necessary on the part of the besiegers to transport supplies of every kind from the Roman camps in the hill country to this almost inaccessible portion of the Dead Sea coast. The nearest water supply was at least eleven miles, and at no point short of twenty miles could a supply of food or forage be secured. In order to conduct a protracted siege—the only possible way of accomplishing his purpose—it was necessary for the Roman general to transport battering rams and siege engines from Jerusalem or the Herodium, and to do this, even in sections, required the construction of a broad roadway, which for a considerable portion of its extent followed the trail of the shepherd or the wild goats, down the rugged mountainside or along the edges of precipitous slopes. When all these difficulties had been surmounted Silva concentrated his army at Masada and commenced the work of investment. His first undertaking after the establishment of his troops in strongly-fortified camps, was the building of a great stone wall around the base of the rock-fortress to prevent the possibility of a sortie or of escape. This wall was connected with the fortified camps, and the security it afforded made it possible for Silva to make use of the greater part of his forces in the construction of a great mound from which he could direct his operation against the wall of the doomed fortress. The only point where it was possible to construct a work of this character was on the west side of the rock, where there is a slight connection,—to which reference has been already made,—between the main ridge and the fortified hill. Upon this under cliff Silva erected an embankment of earth and stone 300 feet in height.

This served as a platform upon which to construct a solid mass of stonework, fifty cubits in breadth and height upon which the siege engines of various kinds were mounted in close proximity to the fortress walls. A great tower, plated with iron, about sixty cubits in height, dominated the wall at this point, also, from which stone and darts were hurled from the engines upon the besiegers, whenever they attempted to defend the walls.

This work of preparation required months of arduous labor, but when the great battering ram began its steady strokes, at close range, from this elevation the walls crumbled before it, day by day, and at length a portion of the rampart, so vigorously assailed, toppled on its foundation and fell to the ground. As the Romans were about to enter this breach they found, to their great amazement, that the beleaguered garrison, in anticipation of this calamity, had erected an inner wall of great strength just behind the portion which had been shattered by the battering rams.

This barrier was constructed of logs and heavy timbers belonging to the palace and other large buildings within the ramparts. These timbers were fitted together in a double framework, and the space between was packed with earth. To prevent the earth from giving way the framework was covered with sloping beams, which bound the whole structure together and gave it greater power of resistance. When the siege engines were directed against this wall there was a rebound from the heavy blows that smote it and the barricade held together as a compact whole. When Silva found that he could not force an entrance in this manner he directed his soldiers to set fire to the woodwork of the barricade. This was accomplished, at length, by hurling torches and blazing bundles of inflammable material upon the roof. The timbers were very dry from long exposure to the heat of this deeply depressed valley, and the flames, which had fastened upon them, spread so rapidly along the hollow framework that it was impossible for the defenders of the wall to extinguish them. At first the heat and smoke from the blazing mass were driven by the wind into the faces of the besiegers, and they almost despaired of success, as the rising flames threatened to overspread the platform upon which their engines were placed, and from which they were preparing to make the final assault. "On a sudden, however," as Josephus puts it, "the wind changed as if it were done by Divine Providence, and blew strongly the contrary way, and carried the flame and drove it against the wall, which was now on fire through its entire thickness. So the Romans, having now assistance from God, returned to their camp with joy and resolved to attack their enemies the very next day."

With the going down of the sun on that eventful day the doom of the heroic defenders of Masada was sealed. They well knew that escape was impossible, and they had little expectation of mercy at the hands of the terrible foemen whom they had so insolently and so persistently defied. To add to the horror of the situation a number of women and children, who had joined their husbands and fathers before the place had been invested, and who had shared with them in all the privations and perils of the long siege, were involved in the same calamity, with the certainty of exposure, now that they were about to be deprived of their protectors, to miseries and indignities more to be dreaded than death itself.

As the barrier which separated the garrison from the dread enemy without was slowly, but surely, settling down into a heap of dust and ashes, Eleazer assembled the entire company and urged them by every consideration of affection and patriotism to devote themselves and all that was within the ramparts to a common destruction. Convinced of the hopelessness of their condition, and aroused to a pitch of frenzy, which brooked no delay, the resolve was made to die together within the walls which they had so heroically defended, rather than submit to the Romans. When everything that was valuable had been gathered together, within and about the palace, and was made ready for the torch, the awful work of self-immolation began. First of all the husbands and fathers tenderly embraced their loved ones, and with unflinching determination put them to death. Then by lot ten men were selected to slay their brethren. When these unresisting victims had fallen by their hands one man, who was chosen in the same manner, slew his nine companions. Standing alone amid this awful carnage the hapless survivor made sure that all in the ghastly funeral pile before him were dead, and then setting fire to the palace and the treasure heaps accumulated around it, ended his life by falling upon his own sword.

Thus perished in that night of horror, which preceded the festival of the Passover, *nine hundred and sixty men, women and children,*—"the last great sacrifice on the altar of Divine retribution."

When the Romans entered the fortress next morning they found in the open space the slaughtered hecatombs of their implacable enemies, lying as they fell and surrounded by heaps of smouldering ruins. As they moved silently and awe-stricken amid this "terrible solitude" they discovered two half-crazed women, and five children who had fled from the scene of slaughter and secreted themselves in one of the vaulted chambers of the enclosure. These were the only persons out of a garrison of nearly one thousand who escaped to tell the tale.

This tragic event took place A. D. 73, seven years after the commencement of the war with Vespasian, and forty years after the crucifixion of Christ.

"This," as one has expressed it, "was the conclusion of the war in which Jerusalem was seen encompassed with armies, the winding up in blood of the drama in which were enacted the scenes of the great tribulation foretold by the Saviour; and terribly to the last, was realized by the devoted people the fearful imprecation of their fathers, 'His blood be on us and our children.'"

Eastward of the ruined site of Machærus, where the plateau of Moab slopes towards the desert the hosts of Israel, under the leadership of Moses and Joshua fought the first great battle for the possession of the promised land. On this side the Jordan Valley, where the wilderness falls away to the Salt Sea the conflict for the last rood of territory in the hands of the descendants of this conquering host was ended at Masada, after a period of occupancy of nearly fifteen centuries. When the news of this final victory reached Rome the province of Palestine was made the private possession of the Emperor Vespasian, and the taxes levied upon it were used for his personal benefit. From that evil day until now the children of Israel have been aliens, with no certain tenure or privilege, in the land of their fathers.

For nearly eighteen centuries after its capture by the Romans Masada was buried in obscurity and its very site was unknown. The first intimation of its possible identification with the great rock, which bore the Arabic name of Sebbeh, was made by our countrymen, Drs. Robinson and Smith, who looked down upon it through a field-glass from a cliff above the fountain of Engedi in the year 1838, but did not have the opportunity to verify their conjecture by the evidence of actual investigation.

In 1842 the place was visited and described for the first time by Messrs. Wolcott and Tipping. Since that date it has been carefully examined and described by such noted explorers as Lieutenant Lynch, De Saulcy, Canon Tristram, General Warren, and the survey party under Kitchener and Conder.

The evidence in support of the identification of this site with Masada is stamped upon every feature of the ruined fortress and its surroundings. There are one or two loosely constructed buildings on the rock which probably represent a brief period of occupancy by hermits or the crusaders, but the surrounding walls, the shells of the Roman camps, and all the rest of the buildings remain as they were left when Silva and his men retired from it. "From the platform," says Colonel Conder, "one looks down on the Roman wall which crosses the plain and runs up the hills to south and north. One can see Silva's camp and the guard towers almost as he left them 1,800 years ago. The Roman mound, the wall upon the ruins of Herod's palace and of the fortress walls, the towers on the cliff side to the north, the empty tanks, the narrow 'serpent' path, all attest the truth of Josephus' account, and remain as silent witnesses of one of the most desperate struggles perhaps ever carried to success by Roman determination, and of one of the most fanatical resistances in history. On the east is the gleaming Sea of Salt; the dark precipices of Moab rise beyond, and the strong towers of Crusading Kerak. On all sides are brown precipices and tawny slopes of marl torrent beds strewn with boulders, and utterly barren shores. There has been nothing to efface the evidence of the tragedy, nor was Masada ever again held as a fortress."

There are many ruins of the past amid the desolations of the Holy Land which claim the attention and stir the emotions of the explorer and traveller, but there is no single monument, perhaps, of the closing period in the history of the Jewish nation that is more interesting and impressive in its surroundings and associations than the huge mass of isolated rock, which bears upon its blackened, blood-stained, storm-swept crest the ruins of Masada.

Index

ABRAHAM, The Friend, 41
Abraham, Oak of, 29
Abraham, Tomb of, 31, 35–39
Adummim, Going up of, 198
Ain el Hod, 196
Ain et Tabighah, 126, 137
Ain et Tin, 100, 125
Akabat ed Deir—outlook from, 198
Aksa El, Mosque of, 149
Amorite Pottery, 22
Amud Wady, 98
Anti-Lebanon, Mountains of, 16
Antonia, Tower of, 157
Apostles, Fountain of, 197
Araunah (Ornan), The Jebusite, Threshing floor of, 165, 172
Attarus Jebel, 226

BANIAS. See Cæsarea Philippi
Bashan, Plateau of, 108
Batihah, Plain of, 113, 130
Belata, 89
Bethabara, 207, 210–212, 222
Bethany (Bethania), Ford of, 211
Bethlehem of Judah, 43
" Approach to, 44
" Fields of, 48
" Basilica of, 51
" Khan of, 50
Bethlehem of Zebulun, 43
Beth-Nimrah, 210
Bethsaida of Galilee, 115, 128

Bethsaida-Julias, 113, 129, 130
Bridge of Jacob's Daughters, 203

CÆSAREA PHILIPPI (Banias), 142–145
Callirhoe (Zerka Main), 227
" Hot springs of, 227–228
Cana (Kefr Kenna), 57, 100
Capernaum, Site of, (Khan Minyeh), 98, 118, 123–126
Capernaum, Fountain of (Ain Tabighah), 101
Capernaum, A Sabbath Day in, 119
Capernaum (Tell Hum), 122
Caravan Routes, 56, 57, 203, 206
Celtic Steamship, Cruise of, 70
Chimham, Khan of, 49
Cisterns, Temple Hill, 153

DALMANUTHA, 115
Damieh Ford, 209
Death, Valley of Shadow of, 73
Decapolis, Cities of, 217
Dome of the Rock, 150
Dothan, Plain of, 19, 20

EDERSHEIM, DR., 66
Egypt, River of, 9
Elijah, Scene of Translation of, 221
Eleazer, Leader of Sicarii, Masada, 237

Engedi, Oasis of, 78
" Fountain of, 78
" City of, 80
" Wilderness of, 78
En Rogel (Spring of Fuller), 181
Ephrath. See Bethlehem
Eschol, Vale of, 29
Et Tell (Bethsaida Julias), 130
Ezekiel, Mystic River of, 75

FOUNTAIN GATE, Jerusalem, 186
Fik, Wady, 114

GALILEE, District of, 64
" Towns of, 114–116
Galilee, Sea of, 107
Galilee, Sea of, Western Shore, 120
Galilee, Sea of, Fisheries of, 110
Galilee, Sea of, Shipping of, 111
Gamala, 114
Gennesaret, Lake of. See Galilee
Gennesaret, Plain of, 97
Gennesaret, Plain, Irrigation of, 102, 103
Gennesaret, Plain, Fertility of, 104
Gennesaret, Plain, Towns of, 114–116
Gennesaret, Plain, Present Condition of, 104
Gergesa (Ghersa), 113
Gerizim, Mount, 93

HAMATH, Entering in of, 9
Haram Area, Jerusalem, 148
" " Walls of, 155
Hattin, Horns of, 100
Hazezon-tamar. See Engedi
Hebron, 27
" Antiquity of, 40
" Mosque of, 32
" Burial Place of Patriarchs in, 32, 34, 35–37

Herod the Great, 226, 235
" " " Works of, 34
Herod Antipas, 228
Herodias, 229, 230
Hermon, Mountain of the Transfiguration, 16, 109, 141–145

JACOB, Well of, 20, 89, 93–95
Jacob, Funeral of, 40
Jericho, The Way to, 193
Jerusalem, 23
" Antiquity of, 22
Jisr el Mejami'a, 205, 220
Jisr Um el Kanatur, 205
John the Baptist, Ministry of, 229
John the Baptist, Prison of, 230
Jordan, Valley of, 16
" River of, 218
" Rapids of, 112
" Fords of, 203
" Perean side of, 206
Joshua, Book of, 12
Joseph, Tomb of, 90

KELT WADY, 74
Khan Minyeh, 98, 122, 125
Kidron, Valley of, 74
King's Garden, Jerusalem, 185

LACHISH (Tell el Hesy), 22
Land and the Book, Correspondence of, 19
Lebanon, Mountain of, 9, 15

MACHÆRUS, Castle of, 225
Machærus, Dungeons of, 231
Machpelah, Cave of, 35
Magdala, 98
Mamre, Vale of, 28
" Vineyards of, 29
Mar Elyas, 44
Maris, Via, 63, 204
Mar Saba, 76
Masada, 225, 232

Index

Michmash, Pass of, 74
Minyeh, Khan of, 98, 122
" Pastures of, 101
Moab, Plain of, 221

NABLUS. See Shechem
Nativity, Church of the, 45, 49, 51, 52
Nativity, Chapel of the, 53
" Cave of the, 51
Nazareth, 55
" Approaches to, 56, 57
" Outlook above, 62
" Village Green of, 56
" Churches of, 58
" Holy Places of, 59
" Fountain of, 60
Neby, Isma'l, Wely of, 62
Nimrim (Nuwaimeh), Ford, 209, 212
Nusairiyeh Mountains, 9

ONOMASTICON, 68

PALESTINE, Greater, 10
" Boundaries of, 12, 13
Palestine, Position among the Nations, 13
Palestine, Unique features of, 13–15
Palestine, Climate of, 17, 18
" Green Pastures of, 21
" Terraced Slopes of, 45
Palestine, Roman Roads in, 56, 57, 203, 206, 218, 233, 238
Palestine Exploration Fund, 11
Papyrus Plant, 101
Patriarchs, Camping Places of, 21
Patriarchs, Burial Places of, 35
" Stone Effigies of, 39
Perea, 206, 214, 220, 229
" Ministry of John the Baptist in, 211, 222, 229

Perea, Ministry of Christ in, 223
Perea, A Jewish Province in the time of Christ, 219
Perea, Pilgrim Route Through, 220

RACHEL, Tomb of, 44
Red Heifer Bridge, Jerusalem, 170
Robinson, Dr. Edward, Explorations of, 11
Robinson's Arch, 156
Roman Roads, 56, 57, 203, 206, 218, 233, 238
Royal Porch, (Herod's Temple), 159

SAKHRA, Sacred Rock of Moriah, 151, 164, 170
Salem. See Jerusalem
Scape Goat, Wilderness of the, 84, 195
Sealed Fountain, 154
Sebbeh. See Masada
Sepphoris, 57
Shechem, City of, 88
" Oldest of the Sacred Places, 88
Shechem, Vale of, 87, 89
" Oak of, 89, 91
Shepherds of Judea, 82, 83
Sichem, Place of. See Shechem
Siloam, Village of, 180
" Pool of, 180
Siloam Conduit, 181
Siloam Inscription, 182
Siloam Pool, Recent Exploration of, 185
Siloam, Old Pool of, 184
St. Stephen, The Sabaite, 76
Sychar, 90
Suweinet Wady, 74

TABERNACLE, Sites of the, 21
Tabor, Mt., 140

Tarichæa, 115
Tell el Amarna Tablets, 22
Tell Hum, 115, 122–125
Temple Area, (Haram), 148
" " Walls of, 23
" " Position of Sanctuary in, 162
Temple Area, Associations Connected with the, 174–178
Temple, Plan of, 158
" Descriptions of, 171–173
" Porches of the, 158, 159
" Sanctuary of the, 160
Tiberias, City of, 115
" Hot Springs of, 115
Transfiguration, Mountain of, 139

VIA MARIS, 63, 204

WADY AMUD, 98
" El Hod, 196
" En Nar, 74

Wady Fik, 114
" Hamam, 98
" Kelt, 74, 197, 198
" Rubudiyeh, 98
" Shaib, 210, 220
" Suweinet, 74
" Tel 'at ed Dumm, 197
" Zerka Main. See Callirhoe
Wilderness of Judea, 72, 81
Wilderness of Judea, Influence of, on Prophets and Poets of Israel, 84
Wilderness, Pastures of the, 81
" Place of John's Preaching, 84
Wilderness, Place of the Temptation, 84
Wilson's Arch, Temple Area, 156

ZIZ, Cliff of, 77

www.ingramcontent.com/pod-product-compliance
Lightning Source LLC
Chambersburg PA
CBHW070235230426
43664CB00014B/2313